T0383938

Team Leadership: How to Define, Apply, and Measure It

A small group of experienced business leaders and academics have teamed up to create an innovative and potentially disruptive approach to developing leadership in the 21st century. The result is a unique, people-centric, and scientifically researched theory of leadership linked to an accurate data-based assessment and diagnostic product. This is the result of several years of study and development as well as many years of curiosity and experience. This is a new approach to leadership development.

The authors use a combination of leadership experience, research, and science to move away from unprovable theory and subjective judgment to deliver a definable product with unlimited application. For individual leaders looking to maximise personal development and results or for organisations wanting to analyse leadership and its effects across an entire structure or business, this book will redefine understanding and development.

The work has proved that team members' perceptions of a leader and leadership behaviours will define their motivation, willingness, loyalty, output, and mental health far more than the actual leadership behaviours themselves. The authors' application of Emergent Team Leadership Theory, why and to what degree team members attribute leadership to their leaders, directors, or managers, leads to accurate assessments of how leaders and leadership are viewed in teams, businesses, and organisations. Importantly, the work is so accurate that individual leaders can define precisely where to focus their personal development to get the most from themselves and their teams. Even for leaders and managers of the same grade in the same role, personal leadership development and training will be different.

This work has developed the Leadership Pathway Audit™ that measures the effectiveness of leadership for any leader or any team and will, over time, chart how leadership changes as any factor of the leader, the team, or the situation changes. Each leader, director, or manager gets a unique representation of the perception of their leadership at any time and a detailed report on the data and perceptions behind this representation. There are limitless options for following this with bespoke analysis of an individual's leadership and for personal development programs tailored to their profile and organisation. Equally, reviewing the entirety of a business or organisation's leadership profiles gives an incredibly accurate view of leadership across an entire company organisation, or sector.

Team Leadership:
How to Define, Apply, and Measure It

Geoff Ribbens, Mark Abraham, and Alistair Cumming

Routledge
Taylor & Francis Group

A PRODUCTIVITY PRESS BOOK

First published 2025
by Routledge
605 Third Avenue, New York, NY 10158

and by Routledge
4 Park Square, Milton Park, Abingdon, Oxon, OX14 4RN

Routledge is an imprint of the Taylor & Francis Group, an informa business

ISBN: 978-1-032-75774-2 (hbk)
ISBN: 978-1-032-75770-4 (pbk)
ISBN: 978-1-003-47556-9 (ebk)

DOI: 10.4324/9781003475569

Typeset in Garamond
by KnowledgeWorks Global Ltd.

Contents

Foreword

All organisations need team leadership, but few objectively measure this key attribute. Most organisations consist of more than one person and therefore need team skills to achieve the desired outcome of the whole being greater than the sum of the parts. Many organisations spend a great deal of money, time, and effort developing leadership and teams but do not measure the results in any meaningful way.

Emergent Team Leadership Theory is a practical way of bringing the challenges of team leadership and achieving high-performing teams closer to reality.

Richard du Plessis

Preface

Who Is the Book For?

This book is invaluable for anyone with a professional or personal interest in one of the most important, yet elusive, aspects of professional and organisational life.

It is an important self-help book for managers, team leaders, project leaders, or any role where you lead and manage a team. Our field research indicates that our approach is exactly what team leaders themselves are looking for.

It is also written for those who guide the assessment and development of team leaders whether as leadership coaches, trainers, consultants, human resource professionals, or those who carry out their performance reviews (appraisals).

It is also an essential reading for all students and lecturers involved in undergraduate and postgraduate courses in sociology, psychology, social psychology, management, and human resource management. All these academic courses cover the concept of 'leadership'.

Our aim has been to develop an approach to team leadership that has **validity** and is also **useful** in ensuring team leaders don't simply 'manage' their team but deliver the 'leadership' the team is looking for. It is an approach that has profound and positive implications for team performance, coaching, training, and performance reviews.

This book on team leadership is unique as it is the only book that defines team leadership in such a way that it can be measured. It is the only book that also shows how leadership emerges in teams. It takes the concept of team leadership to a clearer, more focused level so that it is both academically sound and at the same time, of considerable practical use.

The book is based on a social science perspective where measured results are not black and white, but indicate 'trends', 'pathways', or 'patterns of behaviour'. The data produced comes from team members' *perceptions* of their team leader, based on why the team leader is accepted as their leader and ultimately whether they are 'willingly and enthusiastically accepted'.

Acknowledgements

This book would have not been possible without the help of Richard du Plessis, Andrew Wright MVO; FCIPD, and Alan Garmonsway BSc; FCIPD. All three have used their intellectual skills and experience to add value to the discussion.
   We would also like to thank ….

- Jonathan Ribbens for his computer software skills to create the online Leadership Pathway Audit™.
- Clinton Sturgess who, very early on in our research, asked his team to complete the Leadership Pathway Audit™ about how they perceived him as their team leader. Clinton found the results relevant and powerful.
- Senior leaders in the British armed services who wanted to understand their team's perception of their leadership.
- Adam Lowndes-Knight who manages a local co-op convenience store; he radically improved the store. His small team, when questioned, clearly saw him in terms of our definition of team leadership.
- The mature postgraduate management and HR students at Birkbeck College, University of London, who since 2017, have listened to and critiqued our academic discussion on the concept of leadership.

   And we send our particular thanks to all those team leaders in the organisations we have worked with, who were eager to find out about their team's perception of their 'leadership'. Also feeding back their positive impression of 'Emergent Team Leadership'.
   Whether you are a senior leader in the business or public sector or manage a local store, the approach in this book is relevant. Our approach to team leadership applies to all teams, in all organisations, in all organisational cultures.

About the Authors

Geoff Ribbens MA; BSc; FCIPD; FIoL; PGC ed; PGC coaching

Geoff Ribbens has lectured to postgraduate students in organisational behaviour at several universities: Thames Valley University, Bath University, Oxford Brooks University, Reading University, and Birkbeck, University of London. He has considerable experience in consultancy, training, and coaching in all aspects of organisational behaviour to a wide variety of organisations both public and private. Fifty percent of Geoff's master's degree covered epistemology, the philosophy of science.

Recent Publications.

Understanding Body Language and third edition *Understanding Body Language in Management.* Hodder Education. Geoff Ribbens and Richard Thompson. First edition 2000. Published in USA, Spain, Thailand, France. 2019 in Russian and 2023 in Arabic.

Finding Your Next Job. Hodder Education 2013. Geoff Ribbens and Peter Maskrey.

Geoff.Ribbens@business-enlightenment.com

Mark Abraham OBE

After graduating from The Royal Military Academy Sandhurst Mark had leadership roles in the UK and abroad. A Commanding Officer on operations, his role included MoD policy and as a Colonel, he was Director at the Defence Academy, teaching leadership to the Army's future leaders. He was the British Army's Head of Employment for 3 years before moving back to operational delivery. As a Brigadier he was COO of UK Home Command that covered all UK activity.

Mark led work to advise the US Government on aspects of culture change and lectured at the European Institute on culture change and leadership in large organisations. Mark was a member of the Business in the Community Board for 9 years and was appointed OBE for his work on culture change in 2010.

He subsequently became an NED, director and adviser in the private sector, leading teams delivering key outputs for FTSE 100 and international companies.

A founder of Insight966, Mark has worked with national and international private sector organisations delivering the Leadership Pathway Audit and wider operational, leadership, organisational and culture change development.

Alistair Cumming MSc; FCIPD; FHEA

Alistair draws on over 30 years' experience in learning and development, organisational design, and organisational change roles, working for major organisations across very different industries and cultures, including working internationally at regional and global levels. Professionally, he has extensive experience in the design and delivery of training, formal and informal facilitation of groups, and coaching of individuals. As an interim manager and consultant, he is employed by large and small organisations helping them to implement change and build the skills and capabilities they need for the future. He now blends his time between work within businesses, academia, education, and the voluntary sector. His academic work includes lecturing on MSc and Level 7 programmes. LinkedIn profile at https://www.linkedin.com/in/alistaircumming/.

Chapter 1

The Four Errors That Have Prevented Progress in Our Understanding of Leadership and the Importance of Team Member Perceptions

This chapter is in two parts.

The first part of this chapter looks at the general concept of leadership, with its multitude of different meanings, and why it has held back our understanding of leadership as well as our understanding of 'team leadership'.

The second part of this chapter looks at the importance of team member perceptions and examines previous research about how team members generally evaluate or perceive 'effective' and less 'effective' team leaders.

Part 1: The Weakness of the Current or Traditional Concept of Leadership

The idea of having *leadership* is very attractive. Unfortunately, it has so many different meanings and has never been adequately defined. Journalists tend to use it to refer to those political leaders who they agree

DOI: 10.4324/9781003475569-1

with or admire. Management consultants tend to refer to leadership when it comes to the successful leading or managing organisations and when this equates with business success. Trainers and coaches tend to use the term by referring to team leaders who are seen to be *transformative*; that is, they are associated with the successful introduction of innovation, improvement, and change.

As Kelly (2014) commented: "There has been less progress in leadership studies and leadership coaching in recent years than would be expected from the amount of time, money and effort that has been expended".

We have identified four major reasons, or errors, that account for the lack of progress in the current or traditional approach to leadership. These four errors were initially described by Ribbens et al. (2021).

Error 1: Leadership Is a Quality of the Leader

This first error is simple, and that is the assumption that leadership is some quality or property of the leader.

We see this reflected in Google searches and results: *The 5 things great leaders do every day – the 25 qualities that make for a great leader or 100 things that successful leaders do.*

No such quality or property has ever been, or will ever be, found because what we call 'leadership' actually emerges from people interacting. It is an **emergent social property**, that is, a social property, not a property of the leader. When it comes to 'team leadership', this social property exists in the minds of team members; it is a **perception.**

So, looking at leaders to understand leadership is therefore a fruitless task. Our research has found that it is far more fruitful to look at the team, not the leader, in the search for 'leadership'. This is the logical outcome of seeing leadership as an 'emergent social property'.

Concentrating on some assumed quality or property of the leader is referred to as being 'leader-centric' and has been criticised by Haslam et al. (2011). They comment:

> We consider this individualistic and leader-centric view of leadership to be deeply flawed. It is in many ways, just plain bad: bad in the sense of being a poor explanation of leadership phenomena and bad in the sense of sustaining toxic social realities. (p. 200)

Similarly, Stephen Reicher (professor of psychology at the University of St Andrews, United Kingdom) commented in July 2020: in *The Guardian*, United Kingdom.

> One of the most potent and enduring myths in our society is that leadership is reducible to the power of the leader … such ideas launched numerous studies that sought to find personality characteristics that predict leadership success – none of them particularly fruitful.

As you will see later, our new approach is called Emergent Team Leadership (ETL), and it looks specifically at the leadership of teams. Our emphasis though is more 'team-centric', and we have found that this approach then explains a whole lot more about both team and team leader behaviour.

Error 2: 'leadership' Can Be Universally Applied to Different Contexts

The second error is that understanding 'leadership' involves the same requirements across all social contexts, i.e., 'leadership' of social groups, whole organisations (CEOs), business 'leadership', political 'leadership', and team 'leadership'. From a social science point of view, 'leadership' requires a different definition in each of these areas and certainly needs to be explained through different sociological and social-psychological factors. Having a concept that covers such a broad area tends to lose any explanatory power.

As one finance director commented after we described the second error: "I see, so elephants, trees, travellers and swimmers all have trunks, but the term has different meanings". Although this is an extreme example, it would be better to say that we have 'waves' at sea, radio 'waves', and people who 'wave' goodbye. In such examples, there is a **common pattern**, but they are about **different events**.

Being social scientists, we confine our approach to 'leadership of teams' and no other contexts. ETL avoids the error of lumping different social situations under the same label, the label of *leadership.*

Error 3: Leadership Is Confused With Outcomes

The third error is that leadership as a concept can be judged as good or bad based on its outputs or results. Often these 'good' or 'bad' value judgements are disguised with seemingly harmless terms such as 'good' leadership, 'bad' leadership, 'transformational' leadership, 'servant' leadership, 'authentic' leadership, etc. In the most blatant of cases, definitions of leadership can just mean subjective qualities the writer happens to agree with. The weakness of equating leadership with outcomes which are good, or approved of, such as *transformational* leadership, has been outlined recently by Mats Alvesson (2020). Alvesson points out that it is a value judgement to assume that all leadership must have good outcomes; otherwise, it is not leadership. For example, in our approach, ETL, an Abbot in a monastery may be far from *transformational*, but if he has all the monks 'accepting him', then that is leadership!

Many authors also seem to muddle up what leadership **is** with the mission, purpose, direction, or goal of the leader. This can be seen with reference to transformative leadership, servant leadership, business success leadership, etc. You will never explain what leadership **is**, by confusing it with desired outcomes. As you will see later, ETL separates what leadership **is** from any outcomes – desired or otherwise.

From a social science, or technical, perspective, trying to explain and define leadership by looking at its purpose creates an unscientific 'teleological explanation'. Teleology can be described as trying to explain phenomena in terms of the purpose they serve rather than the cause by which they arise. It is trying to put *effect* before *cause*.

A more scientific or objective approach just concentrates on what *is*, not what *ought to be*. Such an approach may well identify leadership in the most obnoxious, untruthful, politically extreme, and amoral leaders if judged from an outsider's point of view. But science is value-free. It may not tell you what you want to hear; it just tells you what it is, through logic and facts.

So, as you will see, nowhere in our definition of leadership or in our explanation will we refer to 'good' or 'bad' outcomes or outcomes we approve of or disapprove of. Our definition is objective, which is an essential aspect of science. So ETL describes leadership, but it does not concern itself with the direction, strategy, mission, or purpose of the leader or the team.

Once a team leader has *leadership*, within our definition, it is then up to them how they use or misuse it.

Error 4: Leadership Is Poorly Defined

The fourth error is that it is possible to write books and articles on leadership and even run expensive training or coaching programmes without defining precisely what is meant by 'leadership'. It is often used as an everyday word, but it has a multitude of different meanings. Science requires an 'operational definition' of leadership if it is to help to achieve the three aims of science, i.e., *to describe, to explain, and to make forecasts*. An 'operational definition' means that team leadership is directly or indirectly observable and therefore **measurable**.

As you will see later, our approach to team leadership is fundamentally different by taking great care both to define what we mean by the term and to ensure that we do so in a way that we can directly measure and assess it.

Part 2: The Importance of Team Member Perceptions

After much field and desk research, we have identified that to be both effective and valid, any approach to the concept of leadership needs to take away the subjective value judgements and myths that we have seen in Part 1.

As we have seen, looking at the outcomes of leadership, or what writers and others think leaders **ought to do**, is not telling us what leadership **is**. To do this, we also need to concentrate our focus, and our focus, as suggested by the title of this book, is the **leadership of teams** in organisations and in no other leadership contexts.

Furthermore, responding to the leader-centric error noted earlier, we see the critical need to turn the concept of team leadership on its head by pointing out that leadership is not, and never has been, a quality or property of the leader but is instead a perception in the minds of **team members**. More precisely, a perception based on how team members evaluate or judge their team leader.

Team Member Perceptions Matter

All team members, consciously or subconsciously, evaluate, assess, or informally appraise their team leader. This is true whether the person they are assessing is the leader of the executive team or a team leader in a front-line role.

The consequences of this evaluation by the team are often wide-ranging, but a recent Chartered Management Institute report in the United Kingdom (2023) found that: "Workers who rate their manager as ineffective are significantly more likely to be planning to leave the organisation in the next 12 months than those who say their line manager is effective" (p. 6). The report also noted that "31% of managers and 28% of workers have left a job because of a negative relationship with their manager" (p. 13).

In many ways, this is obvious as team member discontent and poor performance can very often be traced back to their relationship with their team leader.

However, building on this point and in response to the four errors of leadership we have just examined, this has led us to recognise that our new theory of leadership needed to concentrate on how team members perceive the nature of their relationship with their team leader. In particular, we needed to understand why team members would accept their leader as a 'leader'; why do team members **accept influence** from their leader, and in what ways do they?

The key difference in our approach to answering these questions though was that whilst other authors have looked at the *supposed properties or qualities of the leader* for an answer, our approach has instead been to seek to understand the perceptions of team members. We are asking a different, more focused question that is 'team member'-centric, not 'team leader'-centric.

Perceptions of Influence and Authority

This team member focus, meant that we needed to understand what forms of influence team members experienced when working for their team leader in organisations – based on their perceptions. This led us to recognise that whilst, of course, any team leader will have influence through the **formal authority** given to them by the organisation, formal authority alone does not lead to team leadership, however we define it. Acceptance by team members is more likely to be based on feelings of respect, wanting to work for their leader, supporting their leader, and perceiving their leader to have professional and technical credibility. Such perceptions can be seen as forms of **informal authority**. The importance of informal authority is that **it is given by the team** to the team leader.

We can differentiate between these two types of authority by saying that authority derived from the organisation is *Formal* Authority, and authority given to the team leader by the team is *Informal* Authority. However, this is a pattern or trend and not necessarily an exact differentiation; social life is seldom clear-cut because formal and informal overlap in organisational settings.

In a different context, David Gergen (2000: p. 65) writes:

> Authority … is more than the formal power that comes from holding office or rank; it is informal power that comes from the respect and deference of others and thus can be infinitely greater in impact.

The essence of different types of authority is based on the reason why team members may accept, or are influenced by, the leader. Haslam et al. states in their preface (2011: p. XX) comment:

> If leadership centres on the process of influence … then, in order to understand it, we need to focus on the mental states and processes that lead people to listen to leaders, to heed what they have to say, and to take on the vision of the leader as their own.

For our own book, we have concentrated on exploring the mental states or perceptions of team members so that we can understand why they are likely to accept the leader's influence/authority.

As we will show later, we have found that informal authority, given to the team leader by team members, is in fact a very powerful form of influence and perhaps the most powerful in creating perceptions of team leadership in the minds of team members. As we will also see later though, it is important to recognise that forms of 'influence' which are seen as acceptable or legitimate will be dependent on context, i.e., the culture of society, the culture of organisations, and the experience and expectations of team members. As we saw from Error 2 earlier, leadership is not acontextual and universal – it is very much situational.

Because the term 'authority' is only generally interpreted as formal authority, we have throughout this book used the term 'influence'. The team leaders' influence in our discussion refers to both formal and very powerful forms of informal authority.

Our Research on Leadership Influence

In our own research, we therefore sought out previous studies that would help us identify those team member perceptions that might correspond to formal and informal forms of influence – whilst asking the key question: *In what ways do team members appear to accept the influence of their team leader?*

When we explored this question, our research involved a detailed examination of the work of many authors and researchers in the field of team leadership over the last six decades. The details of this and our findings can be found in the following chapters; however, the key texts and their influence on our conclusions are summarised below.

Some of these were particularly supportive of the importance of focusing on team member perceptions to understand leadership:

- Meindl et al. (1985) highlighted the 'Romance of leadership' that challenged the leader-centric nature of our view of leadership.
- Haslam et al. (2011) linked leadership to the existence of a shared 'social identity' in the minds of 'followers'.
- Houglum (2012) recognised that leadership *emerges* through the *interaction* of the leader with their team.

Others were particularly helpful in helping us understand what these perceptions of leadership and influence might be based on:

- French and Raven (1959) showed a seminal work on identifying distinct sources of power and influence.
- Bass and Avolio (1990) promoted the distinction between *Transactional* and *Transformational* leadership.
- Goleman (1998) noted that the emergence of 'successful' leadership is when the leader has several capabilities that he classified as *Emotional intelligence*.
- Guirdham (2002) identified factors that 'followers' have in mind when accepting a leader.
- Epitropaki and Martin (2005) highlighted that team members hold implicit beliefs about the traits and abilities that characterise an *ideal* leader.

Whilst other researchers were more generally helpful in showing the value of leaders understanding how they were perceived by their teams and having the opportunity to adjust their own approach following this:

- Fuda (2013) showed the importance of leaders understanding how they are perceived by their teams and getting feedback on this, leading to improved business performance.

In our research and development of our own model of leadership, we have built on the work of others but from a different perspective. We are asking a different question of team members, i.e., **Why do they accept or are influenced by their team leader? Where does the team leader's influence come from in the eyes of team members?**

Our Research Conclusions

As we explain in more detail in Chapter 2, a pattern emerged from our research leading us to identify three broad types of influence perceived by team members.

1. Firstly, the respect team members give their leader in terms of his or her competence or managerial expertise.
2. Secondly, the respect team members give their team leader because team members gain social and emotional rewards from their interaction with their leader.
3. Thirdly, the influence from a transactional relationship between the team members and the team leader, maybe linked to their job title or rank or the financial incentives or practical benefits they can offer.

In other words, team members will tend to evaluate their team leader in terms of his or her management competence or **expertise**, in terms of the social and emotional **rewards** they seem to offer, and in terms of their **transactional** relationship.

We will discuss these three types of influence in more detail in the next chapter.

Notes

We did not want to confuse the reader with two types of **authority**, so we have opted to use the term 'influence' by team members in our discussions. Our definition of influence is a combination of formal and informal authority.

Initially, we used the term 'authority' when it comes to team members' acceptance of their team leader. We defined team leadership as 'a situation where team members willingly and enthusiastically accepted the authority of their leader'. Technically this is correct, but only if you see authority as both formal and informal. Unfortunately, the generally accepted term authority is limited to formal authority, which is given to the team leader by his or her organisation. When it comes to our definition of leadership, it is 'informal authority' based on the leader's expertise or credibility and based on team members gaining social and emotional rewards when working with their leader; that is, the background to 'leadership'.

Chapter 2

Emergent Team Leadership Discovered, Described, Explained, and Measured

Our Definition of Leadership

In developing our own definition and explanation of leadership to address the common leadership errors outlined in Chapter 1, we have aimed to keep our definition simple and easy to understand. We put ourselves in the mind of a team member looking at why they would or would not **accept the influence** of their team leader. In the social sciences, this would lead to a 'meaningfully adequate explanation' of team leadership.

In the literature, generally, discussions of team leadership refer to the importance of having the team accepting the leadership of their leader by pointing out that leadership is not about threats or coercion but about team **acceptance**. This can therefore be seen in our own definition of team leadership:

> Team Leadership is a situation where team members willingly and enthusiastically accept their team leader.

The theme and emphasis of this book are based on team members and their perceptions, not on the team leaders themselves. However, once the team leader is aware of how he or she is perceived by team members, that leader can consider ways to improve their relationship with their team, and

DOI: 10.4324/9781003475569-2

indeed, our unique approach then shows the **pathway** team leaders can take to improve this relationship.

The Principles of Emergent Team Leadership

To understand our approach, which we refer to as **Emergent Team Leadership** (ETL), we need to outline certain principles:

1. Leadership emerges from the leader and the team interacting. From a social science perspective leadership is an 'emergent social property', it is **not** the property of the leader, but instead exists as a perception in the minds of team members.
2. Leadership is an accepted form of influence that exists in team members' perceptions, which we can define and measure. There are formal forms of influence, such as a leader's job title, and informal ones, such as the leader's managerial expertise or the social and emotional rewards experienced by team members when they work closely with their leader.
3. Leadership emerges when team members perceive their leader both as a competent manager (meaning that the leader has some degree of managerial knowledge, skill, and expertise) and when team members feel that they gain social and emotional rewards from interacting with their leader. This is typically where the 'enthusiasm' comes from in our definition.

Our Three Forms of Leadership Influence

As we noted in Chapter 1, we have identified the three most accepted forms of influence experienced and expected by team members. We use the expression 'accepted influence' because there are a multitude of influences based on team members' perceptions, but we only concern ourselves with those influences in organisational life that are legitimate or socially acceptable.

1. **Expert influence**. This is the influence based on the team leader's perceived competence or **expertise** as a manager. Here, in team members' eyes, the team leader knows what they are doing and where they are going – and so has **credibility** in the eyes of team members.

2. **Reward influence**. This is the influence based on the social and emotional **rewards** expected and experienced by team members, such as feeling motivated, sharing social and work values, and feeling their team leader cares about them and their work.

3. **Transactional influence**. This is the influence based on a **transactional** relationship. Here team members accept the influence of their leader because of his or her job title or the fact that the leader offers extrinsic incentives or benefits of some kind.

All three of these influences are important in determining how team members perceive the leadership of their team leader and whether they will 'willingly and enthusiastically accept them' in line with our definition stated above.

Expert, Reward, and Transactional Forms of Influence Expanded

For each of the three forms of influence identified above, we drew on our research of the work of previous authors to develop 12 commonly defined areas of acceptable influence.

■ Four common forms of expert influence
■ Four common forms of social and emotional rewards influence
■ Four common forms of transactional influence

The sources for these 12 forms of influence are explained more fully in Chapter 6. However, it is clear from our research that these 12 forms of influence are frequently referred to, although not in the same way, by many other authors as qualities or properties of the leader. Indeed, many previous approaches have asked employees about 'good' or 'bad' leaders they have experienced, and such surveys support the 12 forms of influence which we have described.

But our approach is different. As we have noted already, many authors make the error of moving from what is clearly a perception by employees to assuming that such perceptions are qualities of the leader. Our approach sees 'team leadership' simply as a perception of team members, not some quality of the leader themselves.

In our model, the **essence** of team leadership **emerges** when team members gain social and emotional rewards when interacting with their team leader. This outcome is often associated with team members perceiving their leader as having credible or the appropriate expertise.

Transactional forms of influence are often linked to formal forms of authority, that is, authority given to the team leader by the organisation. Clearly, formal authority can have an impact on the emergence of leadership. That impact can be supportive of the emergence of leadership or can be negative when it comes to the team member gaining social and emotional rewards. See the typical forms of transactional leadership below.

ETL is thus concerned with identifying **patterns** of team leader **behaviour as perceived** by team members across these three areas of influence.

Each of these three areas of influence is now unpacked further in more detail below.

Team Leader Influence Based on Their Perceived Expertise

Here, team members willingly accept the influence of their team leader because they perceive the team leader as having expertise such that they are perceived as a competent manager. The four elements of team leader expertise we outline are:

1. **Confidence**. The team leader is perceived by team members to be confident in their role and the decisions they make. The leader tackles difficult issues in a confident manner and they are persuasive when presenting ideas.
2. **Organisation and sector knowledge**. The team leader is perceived by team members to have knowledge of their own organisation and the sector or environment it operates in. So, for example, the CEO in the executive team has knowledge of the wider environment, whilst the team leader in a manufacturing context understands his or her team's relationship with other teams or departments.
3. **Organising/administrative skills**. The team leader is perceived by team members as competent at organising and administration generally and skilled at planning and organising team members.
4. **Technical or professional expertise**. The team leader has the appropriate technical or professional skills and knowledge associated

with their role. This means that they will better understand the work and resources team members require and provide technical or professional feedback to team members as required.

Team Leader Influence Based on Social and Emotional Rewards

Here, team members find interacting with their team leader psychologically or socially rewarding. As we are concerned with 'perceptions', it is important to remember that it is the team members who define what is **rewarding** for them based on their expectations and experience. The four common types of social and emotional Rewards we outline are:

5. **Motivation**. Team members find that interacting with the leader meets their motivational requirements. Team members feel empowered and responsible. They have a sense of achievement, and their aptitudes and skills are recognised by the team leader.
6. **Trainer/coach**. Team members feel that their leader is interested in their training, coaching, and development. The team leader encourages them to learn new things and shares their own knowledge and experience with team members. Team members feel they are learning from their team leader, even if it is in an informal way.
7. **Agent of beneficial change**. Team members perceive their team leader as introducing or supporting what they see as beneficial change. Again, this assessment is in the eyes of team members. It might include helping them secure their jobs or introducing more interesting work. Here, team members are encouraged to improve what they do, and new ideas from team members are encouraged.
8. **Shared vision and values**. Team members share the same work vision and social values, principles, and goals as their team leader and perceive their team leader as treating them fairly and as individuals. Here also, team members feel they, as individuals, matter – at least as much as measures of productivity and performance.

Team Leaders Influence Based on Their Transactional Relationship

In all organisations, there are elements of influence that a team leader can draw on that relate to the authority they are given by the organisation through the position or role they are appointed to, the resources they have available, and what is formally expected of them by the organisation. As with all the eight areas of influence mentioned already, what matters is how these transactional forms of influence are perceived by the team members. As we will discuss later in this book, organisational culture has a big influence here as to what is viewed by team members as acceptable or indeed expected. We can see below that transactional forms of influence can have a positive impact or negative impact on the emergence of leadership. See note on transactional influence at the end of this chapter.

The four elements of transactional influence are:

9. **Extrinsic incentives**. Team members accept the influence of their team leader because the team leader provides or influences the provision of tangible and valued incentives, for example, monetary rewards. In some organisational cultures, such as banking, individual bonuses would be a common example here. However, in most contexts, a front-line team leader's influence on pay will be more limited, so their influence will be more through indirect incentives such as allowing time off when needed, access to overtime or better-quality work, or more broadly, the positive performance assessment rating or promotion recommendation they can award.

10. **Fear/anxiety**. Here, team members might accept the influence of their team leader due to fear or anxiety, such as fear of the consequences of disagreeing with or disobeying their team leader. Deliberately creating fear or coercion in the team and team leader relationship is not acceptable and is not a form of accepted influence, although team leaders may threaten, or even use the disciplinary procedures (corrective procedures) as a form of influence. However, as noted above, each team member may perceive their team leader very differently. The team leader themselves may not realise that they are perceived by team members in a manner that involves fear or anxiety on the part of team members.

11. **Position**. Team members accept the influence of their team leader because of their job title, position in the organisation, or rank. Sometimes this is referred to as 'formal authority' because it is given to the team leader by the organisation, not by team members. A team leader may also have influence because they are close to more senior or influential leaders. In the emergency services, rank or job title as

a form of influence is expected and indeed willingly accepted in the relationship between team members and team leaders.

12. **Controlling**. Team members may accept that they can be told what to do by their team leader and so expect to just follow instructions. This is like the 'position' influence above, except here the influence is coming from the organisational systems and processes that require compliance and conformity. Again, different organisational cultures will have different expectations here, and this will impact the expectations of team members as to what is appropriate. Individual team leaders though can overdo this form of influence, by, for example, concentrating too much on team member errors and omissions, perhaps creating a blame culture. Similarly, micromanaging might be acceptable when dealing with new team members but can be very demotivating for more experienced team members.

One example of controlling, as in micromanaging, we came across was an engineering manager who was trying to help a team member repair a machine. In the mind of the manager, he was trying to help, but in the mind of the team member, he was unnecessarily interfering.

Measuring Leadership

O wad some Power the giftie gie us; to see oursels as ithers see us!

(Burns, 1785)

How others see us can be a revelation, so it is important that the leader finds out how team members perceive them. We are particularly interested in how the team member perceive them as leaders and not wider perceptions about their personality, lives, or any other interesting but relatively irrelevant aspects.

Very few leaders have a clear understanding of how their own team perceive their leadership. From our research, we have been able to develop a diagnostic instrument (see below) which creates a profile for a leader that is far more accurate and less subjective than being verbally questioned by a team leader or coach or taking part in focus groups. Furthermore, it connects back to and is based around a specific definition of leadership.

How We Measure Team Members' Perceptions: The Leadership Pathway Audit™

Now that we have defined and explained the 12 forms of Influence available to team leaders, we can now explore the diagnostic instrument we have developed to measure the emergence of leadership in any context – the Leadership Pathway Audit™ (LPA).

This is an *audit* because it measures team members' perceptions of their leader's influence, and it is a *pathway* because it shows leaders what they need to do to change those perceptions if that is required, so they can move along the *pathway* towards *leadership*.

Features of the LPA

Our diagnostic instrument, the LPA, is a carefully designed online diagnostic tool.

- Team members are asked how they perceive influential behaviours exhibited by their team leader. These relate to the 12 acceptable forms of influence we have defined above.
- Behind each of the 12 forms of influence, we described earlier, there are five elements or examples. Looking at the 12 forms of influence and all the underpinning factors in different ways reduces biases or misunderstandings and provides greater clarity and detail.
- From the point of view of team members, the LPA is about their perception of their team leaders' influencing style and is completely anonymous. It does not ask them to criticise, praise, judge, or write any kind of subjective description.
- We have not included the term 'leadership' in the diagnostic tool as the term might distort their response so this is never used. After all, academics and experts seem to disagree about what 'leadership' means, so why should we expect ordinary team members to come up with a common definition?
- Once completed by all team members, the LPA report provides a detailed view of each team member's perceptions but also an aggregation of the views of all team members to create the leader's profile as a visual radar graph that depicts the 12 influences described above.

Let's now look at an example radar graph (Figure 2.1).

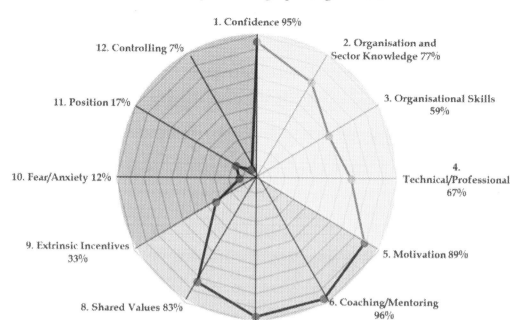

Figure 2.1   Team leader with strong leadership profile

Background Context

This was a senior leader responsible for leading other team leaders within a large organisation. The departments were teams of specialists delivering different outputs all of which were required for the organisation to succeed professionally and commercially. Some departments were technical and relied on functioning equipment and the skill to utilise technology competitively. Others were people- and HR-based, requiring people skills, interaction with stakeholders and a customer focus. Other departments were internal management and co-ordination as well as finance and accounting.

This background helps to explain the profile that you can see for this leader in Figure 2.1.

The Results

■ The scores for **expertise** were lower than the scores for **reward** because the team members of this team were the heads of smaller departments, and these departments were to some degree teams of specialists; they were certainly responsible for specific functions. The senior leader did not have expertise in the work that all the other smaller departments did, and this is reflected in the relatively lower but still quite high score for technical and professional knowledge.

■ The profile indicates that team members feel that the leader is creating a **rewarding** workplace or culture, and that the leader's behaviour leads to team members feeling motivated and all the elements that lead to socio-emotional rewards; they appear to like working for this leader.

■ For the **transactional** attributes, this leader had very low perceptions of leading by using or relying on their position or by excessive controlling or creating a level of fear or apprehension in the team members. Interestingly, the scores for these attributes were not zero. The score of 33% for extrinsic incentives, such as individual bonuses, etc., reflected that such incentives were part of the team or organisational culture.

How to Interpret Profiles

It is important to look at any profile holistically to assess whether it meets our definition of leadership, i.e., **a situation where team members willingly and enthusiastically accept their team leader**.

Given this definition, in our approach to team leadership, we are suggesting that such a leadership situation will emerge under some combinations of the following conditions …

Team members perceive strong social and emotional rewards, the essence of leadership:

■ Where team members find interacting with their leader is motivational.
■ Where team members perceive their leader to be interested in their training, coaching, and development.
■ Where the team leader is seen to encourage beneficial change, i.e., change which is perceived to be beneficial by team members.
■ Where team members perceive the team leader as sharing their social and work values.

Team members perceive strong expert or managerial competence:

■ Where the team leader is perceived to be confident in their role.
■ Where the team leader is perceived to have knowledge of the organisation or sector it operates in.

- Where the team leader is perceived to be organised and on top of administration.
- Where the team leader is perceived to have the appropriate technical and professional skills as well as understanding the work of the team.

A transactional relationship can have a neutral or positive impact on the emergence of leadership under the following conditions:

- Where the team leader is perceived to be fair in their use of extrinsic reward.
- Where the team leader is perceived to act appropriately in terms of their position in the organisation.
- Where the team leader is perceived to act appropriately in terms of their use of controls over work and processes.
- Where the team leader is not seen to overly rely on producing fear or anxiety amongst team members.

This last area especially highlights that when interpreting the results of any audit you need to understand the **background context** and indeed look at the individual scores of all the team member respondents to check for disparities of views across the team as well as any outliers that might have distorted the overall results.

Conclusions on the Radar Graph Example

From the last section, we see that the **essence** of team leadership is based on team members experiencing social and emotional rewards when interacting with their team leader and being perceived by team members to have expert forms of influence that give the team leader credibility in their eyes.

The link between perceived reward and perceived expert forms of influence is obvious for all of us who have been team members or even team leaders – and as such can be seen as *meaningfully adequate* as an explanation. The two forms of influence tend to go together.

If we now look back to the radar graph, we saw in Figure 2.1, we will draw your attention to the very high levels of social and emotional rewards that team members appear to be gaining from interacting with this team leader. Scores of 89% for motivation, 96% for coaching/mentoring, 96% for agent of change, and 83% for shared values are all very high. We don't have here the individual team member scores, so we cannot say how universal this regard was across all forms of influence. However, in the rewards area at least, the very high average scores would suggest that this is a commonly held view by the team.

Despite the relatively lower scores for expertise, these high scores for social and emotional rewards would suggest that team members are accepting their team leader and perhaps doing so 'enthusiastically'. The fact that they do not appear to be relying on transactional influences is also interesting and would certainly be explored in the feedback.

As a general guide high scores for transactional forms of influence or even high scores for expert forms of influence and low scores for social and emotional rewards indicate that the leader is lower down the pathway to team leadership.

Applying the Leadership Pathway Audit™

The Leadership Pathway Audit Is Not Just Another 360-Degree Assessment

It is common these days to promote the benefits of 360-degree appraisals, often comparing results between employees including team leaders. This is useful when looking at how team members, colleagues, senior managers, customers, and other stakeholders perceive an individual leader. However, a 360-degree approach is unsuitable for looking at the perceptions of team leadership as we have defined it in this book. It is only team members that perceive their leader in terms of influence (both formal and informal) linked to team leadership.

Our diagnostic tool, the LPA, is more in-depth than a traditional 360 appraisal and the results are more powerful. Our field research case studies (see Chapter 3) indicate that it is also more relevant in the eyes of team leaders than 360-degree approaches the participants had previously experienced. Leaders can sometimes dismiss their 360 results by pointing out that all the people surveyed 'do not really know them'. However, they have no excuse with an influence profile which is generated by their own team.

Working With the Results – To Change Perceptions

Psychometric tests are often perceived by many as fixed, such that a team leader cannot change their personality. But the LPA is not a psychometric and the results are not fixed. When feeding back therefore, we believe it is important to emphasise to the team leaders that the LPA results only refer to one moment in time, i.e., they are the current perceptions of their team. As such, if the results are not what they hoped for, they can be encouraged by the fact that those perceptions can be changed – if the team leader wants to put in the work to change them. Equally though, they need to avoid complacency if their results look very favourable – the perceptions of their team can change, just as contexts can change.

As we will see in Chapter 4, the approach we are taking is therefore powerful in training, coaching, appraising and can also be useful when it comes to 'self-development'. Team member perceptions can be changed – once you know what they are.

Many leaders may acquire information about the leadership in books, on MBA programmes or on training programmes, but rather less commonly 'on the job'. Yet as Moldoveanu and Narayandas (2019) in the Harvard Business Review comment:

> Research by cognitive, educational, and applied psychologists dating back a century, along with more recent work in the neuroscience of learning, reveals that the distance between where a skill is learned (the locus of acquisition) and where it is applied (the locus of application) greatly influences the probability that the student will put that skill into practice. (p. 8)

This highlights that the greater that distance, the less likely that any new learning will be applied. So, the challenge in helping team leaders learn about leadership is to find ways to reduce this distance and bring the learning closer to its place of application, i.e., the workplace itself. This is what the LPA offers by helping team leaders learn directly about how their own team perceives their leadership in the workplace and from this insight learn some of the steps they can take to directly influence those perceptions.

Summary

ETL theory is simple. Leadership is defined as a 'social situation where team members willingly and enthusiastically accept their leader'. The necessary conditions which are jointly sufficient for leadership to emerge in organisations can be seen as a pattern or trend identified by the LPA.

The essence of team leadership resides in social and emotional rewards. Such socio-emotional rewards are nearly always linked to the team leader being perceived in terms of credibility. In some team leadership situations, a pattern might emerge which might also include some transactional perceptions such as the importance of position or extrinsic incentives.

The way to think about ETL is to think like a team member. As a team member, you might just accept the influence of the leader if it is **only** based on a transactional relationship. You might willingly accept that influence if it is **only** based on the leader's expertise, and you might willingly and enthusiastically accept that influence if it is based on social and emotional rewards and associated credibility or expertise.

We recognise that in some social and organisational cultures, team members may gain social and emotional rewards from certain transactional forms of authority. But we suggest that in most organisations something more is needed.

We have identified 12 common forms of influence as perceptions in the minds of team members. Nearly all these forms of influence have been mentioned by other scholars of leadership (see Chapter 6) but are often assumed to be qualities or properties of the leader. We have merely turned it around to see them as perceptions of team members.

In the next chapter, we are going to discuss some case studies based on ETL and LPA.

Notes on Transactional Forms of Influence

A good example of position influence is rank or job title; it is one of the five examples of position influence. In the emergency services, rank is an indication of knowledge, skills, experience, and credibility and therefore positive to the emergence of leadership. If, however, the only influence or authority a team leader has, in the eyes of team members, is their rank or job title then this is a negative sign for the emergence of leadership.

Chapter 3

Case Studies Based on Emergent Team Leadership and the Leadership Pathway Audit™

Introduction

In this chapter, you will see several case studies profiling team leaders who took part in our field research of the Leadership Pathway Audit (LPA). During this process, the team leaders asked their team members to complete the Audit in a confidential and anonymous way. We, as researchers, analysed the results and then fed them back to the team leaders in a one-on-one session.

The Process Followed

The LPA looks at 60 elements that track back to the 12 forms of influence that we discussed in Chapter 2, i.e., shared values, confidence, coaching/mentoring, etc. Each form of influence is measured against five key elements.

Once completed by all team members, a profile was created that aggregated the scores of all the respondents expressed as a percentage against each form of influence. The individual breakdown of each of the team members was also available to the researcher feeding back on the profile so that they could see the range of scores, derived from team member responses and note any outliers.

The resulting analysis was highly detailed so that the team leader, or those giving feedback, could focus on responses or percentage scores that interested or concerned them. In the feedback sessions with the team leader, specific reasons for the percentage scores could be discussed under each of the 12 headings. With these prompts, further discussions took place around their own specific context, and additional insights were gained by the leader as we will explain below.

Interpreting the Results

The case studies illustrate how the team leaders themselves gained new insights from identifying their team members' perceptions of their 12 forms of influence.

We suggested in Chapter 2 that to meet our definition of team leadership the essence of team leadership will be found when team members gain social and emotional rewards from interacting with their leader. This would enhance their 'enthusiasm' for accepting their leader. We also suggested that such rewards would be dependent on the team's perception of their leader's credibility or managerial expertise – this being key to them accepting their influence in the first place. We therefore expected to find a positive relationship between reward influence and expert influence when it comes to the development of leadership.

We also considered how transactional forms of influence might impact perceptions of leadership as these we expected to be more dependent on the culture and context of the organisation and the specifics of that particular situation. For example, in a culture of formality and status based on job title or rank, we might expect more acceptance of this influence (and hence higher scores for these elements). Equally, we might also expect that team members would describe a new leader in terms of transactional forms of influence as team members have yet to see evidence of their expert and reward forms of informal influence.

In examining the data produced by the LPA and discussing this with the team leaders in the feedback sessions, our aim was to identify those factors that help an individual team leader move along the *pathway* towards team leadership, whilst recognising the specific context and situations they found themselves in. We recognise that one case study, in-depth, would probably fill up a whole chapter; so for this reason, the case studies below will just focus on the main issues arising, although we have deliberately chosen some distinctly different cases to draw out a wide range of points that illustrate the value and insights gained by the leaders.

Whilst each case needs to be viewed in its own context, our guiding question, at all times, needs to be: Does the evidence gathered from the perceptions of their team members suggest that there appears to be 'a situation where (those) team members willingly and enthusiastically accept their team leader?'

Case Study Examples

CASE STUDY 3.1: 'MOVING ALONG THE PATHWAY TO TEAM LEADERSHIP'

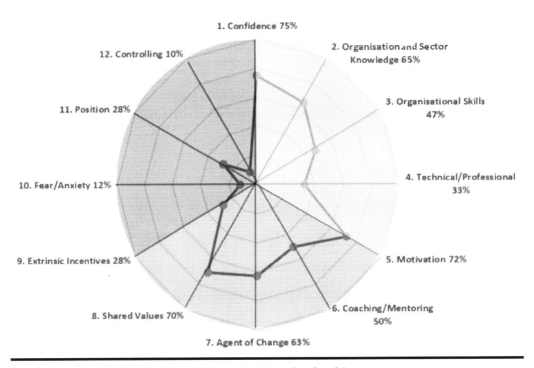

Figure 3.1   Moving along the pathway to team leadership

BACKGROUND

This profile is of a senior leader responsible for several other team leaders with smaller teams and with some team members who worked directly for them with no team. This is a very typical profile where team members have their own expert knowledge and skills. The leader was considered by the team to be a 'really nice person', who was a good team leader and who it was nice to work for.

INTERPRETING THE FINDINGS

As you can see in Figure 3.1, the team seem to have a generally positive perception of this leader when it comes to their feeling motivated (5) when working with this leader (72%). They also seem to share the same values (8) as their leader (70%). However, coaching and mentoring (6) scored only 50%, which would suggest that the team seemed less inclined to go to their leader for advice or support about work-related issues. In fact, the leader was in a role where most of the team were quite senior and experienced and did not want or require coaching/mentoring. Team members only scored 33% for the leader's technical and professional expertise (4). The reason for this, again, was that the team members were already experts in their particular roles and did not expect the team leader to also be an expert in the work that they carried out.

The team were more interested in the team leader's role in providing strategic decisions and output-based targets. Team members may have learnt from interacting with their leader, not just about their own expertise, but where their role fits into the bigger picture.

Those giving feedback to the team leader might mention the high scores for motivation and shared values and then explore areas that might be of concern to the team leader. It is always helpful in any discussion to start with the positive.

In terms of the (blue) area of expertise, the team leader was perceived as having a reasonable level of organisation and sector knowledge (2) with a score of 65%, and score breakdown by question suggested that team members recognised that the team leader understood the bigger picture. Again, this score could still be improved further by the leader reminding team members of that bigger picture in meetings and discussions.

However, the team leader scored only 47% for organisation and administration (3), which might suggest an area where the team leader needed to improve in the eyes of team members. Poor scheduling and administration can let the team down and cause problems for members.

The transactional score was 28% for position (11) and extrinsic incentives (9). These scores could be explored with the team leader, but it might well be that such scores are expected in this organisations culture. As noted above, we always need to place the data generated by the LPA in the social context of the team and organisation. The low scores on position particularly and the very low scores on fear/anxiety (10) and controlling (12) would though suggest that the team leader does not appear to rely on these forms of influence in the eyes of their team members.

Conclusions and Insights

Figure 3.1 indicates that the team leader is perceived by their team to be well on the *path* of leadership. In the feedback, he considered that this was the most accurate assessment of him, his team, and his leadership that he had received despite having been in the organisation for nearly 30 years and having taken part in many traditional leadership and personality assessments.

CASE STUDY 3.2: A CONFIDENT TEAM LEADER WHO CAN SEE THE BIGGER PICTURE

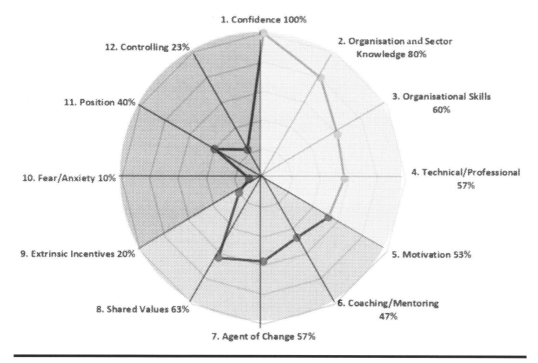

Figure 3.2   A confident team leader who can see the bigger picture

BACKGROUND

This was a leader in a similar role to the one we have just described (in Case Study 3.1) with a similar set of responsibilities and a similarly sized and diverse team.

INTERPRETING THE FINDINGS

In this case, the leader scored higher across the board for their expert attributes and was perceived by the organisation to be ideally suited to leading that team. It is worth noting that the score for confidence (1) is often seen by an organisation as a measure of 'leadership' or 'leadership potential', and in this case, their team members scored them 100%, whilst the team leader in the previous case study had 75% for the same form of influence.

However, although the team leader in this case had higher levels of expertise, as perceived by team members, their scores for two socio-emotional rewards were, in comparison, lower. For example, motivation (5) scored 53%, shared values 63%, and agent of change 57%. Coaching/mentoring (6) scored just 47%, but this can be explained because team members were already experts and did not turn to the team leader for coaching or mentoring.

The scores in this case study would suggest that the team leader could explore ways to improve their team members perceptions when it comes to social and emotional rewards, especially motivation.

Here, more in-depth exploration and feedback looking at all the issues behind the 12 forms of influence can provide some helpful potential answers.

As you will see in Figure 3.2, the team leader in this case had slightly higher scores for the transactional dimensions of controlling (23%) and position/rank (40%) compared with the team leader in Case Study 3.1 who scored only 10% and 28%, respectively. In the analysis and feedback discussions, it would be worth exploring whether, even with these relatively low scores, team members might be feeling that their leader is over-controlling and relying too much on their position authority and how this is then impacting their employees' motivation (5).

CONCLUSIONS AND INSIGHTS

The data create many questions for the individual team leader to explore and provide a multitude of questions ideally suited to the coaching or training process.

As an example of the accuracy of Emergent Team Leadership (ETL), as well as the relevance for specific teams, it is worth looking at the score for controlling. We review five elements of controlling including leadership behaviour that creates a blame culture or is inflexible. One of the elements looked at is micromanagement. In this case, although the score for controlling was only 23%, the score for micromanagement, which is one-fifth of the total for controlling, was 90% with single-figure scores for the other four elements. The results enable the leader to explore with the team why, when he believed he gave the team members the freedom to achieve results using their own initiative and approach, they perceived that he micromanaged them.

CASE STUDY 3.3: WHY HIGH SCORES FOR POSITION AUTHORITY AND FEAR/ANXIETY NEED NOT HAVE A NEGATIVE IMPACT ON SOCIAL AND EMOTIONAL REWARDS

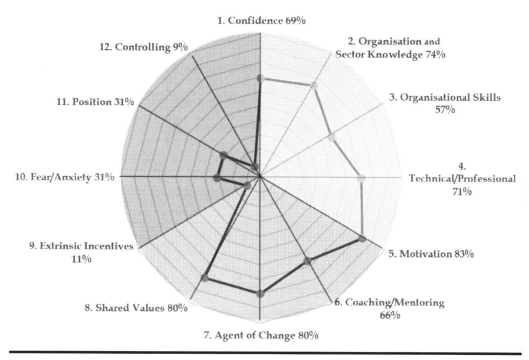

Figure 3.3 Why high scores for position authority and fear/anxiety need not have a negative impact on social and emotional rewards

BACKGROUND

This is a case study of a leader in a different organisation and sector but with a similar role at a similar grade or level of management to those in the first two case studies.

INTERPRETING THE FINDINGS

Scores for shared values (8) at 80%, agent of beneficial change (7) at 80%, and motivation (5) at 83% suggest strong indications of enthusiasm by team members towards their team leader (Figure 3.3). In comparison, coaching and mentoring (6) scored just 66%, but like the other two case studies, the team were already experienced and experts in their role. Team members were still learning from the team leader but about the bigger picture not about their own skills specialism.

What is interesting is that, at the same time, the team perceived this leader as relatively high at 31% for fear and anxiety (10). This would be worth exploring in the feedback session. Perhaps, for example, the leader has recently had to use disciplinary procedures within the team or there are fears of redundancies. This highlights the potential importance of context. In parallel, their score for position authority (11) was also relatively high at 31%. However, it is equally interesting to note that neither of these relatively high scores seemed to have significantly impacted team member motivation, shared values, or the leader being perceived as an agent of beneficial change.

This highlights again that the transactional scores need to be viewed and understood in a wider context. For example, position or rank is important in the emergency services and not necessarily perceived by team members to be negative as a form of influence. Team members in such contexts tend to respect rank or position as it is believed to signify knowledge and experience.

The LPA profile will explain the relationship between the highish scores for position and fear/anxiety as perceived by team members. It might not be that this team leader is viewed by their team as falling back on their position (rank) and/or using fear/anxiety to exercise their authority and influence. Linked to this, the leader might be using position/rank (31%) and fear/anxiety (31%) to back up the introduction of change which scored 80%. It could be that a minority of team members do not support the specific change, so the leader feels he/she needs to fall back on more formal methods of influence. These issues will be discussed in the feedback session.

Conclusions and Insights

The positive profile of this leader in terms of social and emotional rewards should improve the leader's confidence after the feedback. This is a clear case of a leadership profile.

The Next Two Case Studies Indication That the Team Leader Wants to Improve the Team's Performance

The two case studies that follow, 3.4 and 3.5, illustrate what ETL and the LPA tell us about the team and the team leader. They also tell us what emerges from the feedback to the team leader. We are using Case Study 3.4 (Figure 3.4) to show where team leadership has yet to emerge and why the team leader responded to the team in the way they did. In Case Study 3.5, we have a team leader who is perceived by their team in many different ways but the clear trend is towards our definition of leadership. In both our examples, we have selected leaders who had 'difficult' poorly performing teams – in the eyes of the team leader. The team leader also described individual poor performers and the need for such things as team building.

CASE STUDY 3.4: THE TEAM'S PERCEPTION IS THAT OF A MAINLY TRANSACTIONAL RELATIONSHIP NOT LEADERSHIP

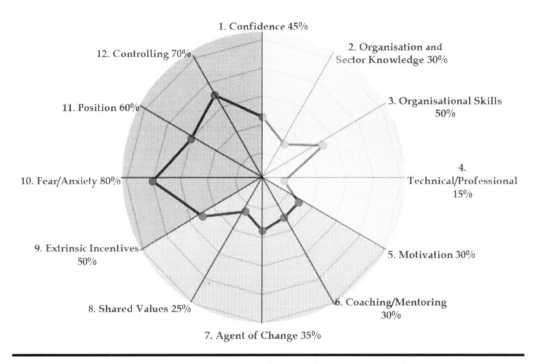

Figure 3.4 The team's perception is that of a mainly transactional relationship not leadership

BACKGROUND

This was a good example of a team who did not yet strongly perceive their team leader in terms of 'team leadership'. This was a new team leader who had taken over the team just recently, so their influence/authority is based mainly on transactional forms. This is to be expected for any new team leader. It was also the team leader's first team leader role, and unfortunately, for them, the team had some very poor performers. Another added problem was the team leader had very little previous knowledge about the activities or work of the team (technical and professional knowledge of the team's work was only 15%). The team leader in this case wanted to improve the performance of the team but given their limited time in the role only had transactional or formal forms of influence available.

INTERPRETING THE FINDINGS

Their very high score of 80% for fear/anxiety (10) was perhaps linked to the context where the leader was needing to correct and discipline some poorly performing team members. They also had to use their position/rank (11) as a form of influence (reflected in their score of 60%). Poor performance also meant that the team leader felt they needed to direct and control (12) team members and tell individuals what is expected of them (reflected in a 70% score for controlling).

Their average score for social and emotional rewards was 30%, which may suggest some hope that this leader was starting on the *pathway* to team leadership. Given the context, as they develop further in the role, they could try to strengthen team members' perceptions of reward. The team leader might try to introduce change and improvements (7) by showing how it will benefit team members and go out of their way to fully understand the work of the team, technical and professional skills (4), and the development needs of their team (6).

CONCLUSIONS AND INSIGHTS

We learned from this case that it is not recommended or ideal to use the LPA on very new team leaders. Such leaders have yet to establish themselves and for the team to form clear perceptions of their progress against all 12 forms of influence. It was though still interesting and useful to see this context reflected in the profile created and to signal to the team leader the areas that they would need to focus on in the next phase of their development in the role.

CASE STUDY 3.5: TRANSFORMATIONAL LEADERSHIP WITH A POORLY PERFORMING TEAM

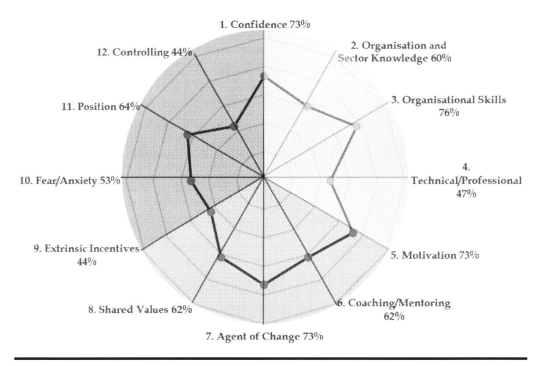

Figure 3.5   Transformational leadership with a poorly performing team

BACKGROUND

This team leader had been in their role for five months and had taken responsibility for a very poorly performing and dysfunctional team. The team leader was tasked with improving the team's productivity and performance and turning the team around.

INTERPRETING THE FINDINGS

The team leader was not an expert in the activities of all the individual team members, and this is represented in the relatively low score of 47% for technical and professional knowledge and skill (4). He had, however, in previous months, gone out of his way to work closely with team members, so he understood their role and the problems and difficulties they had. This does seem to be reflected in the team members' perceptions of his coaching and mentoring (6), which was scored at 62%.

Scores for motivation (5) at 73%, agent of change (7) at 73%, and shared values (8) at 62% suggest that the team leader was perceived by their team as providing social and emotional rewards, suggesting some enthusiasm for his leadership. Even the scores for expert knowledge and skills perceived by team members were high under the circumstances. Score for confidence (1) was 73%, organisational and sector knowledge (2) was 60%, and organisation and administration (3) was 76%.

However, instead of seeing lowish scores for transactional influences, as we have seen in most of the previous case studies, we see here in Figure 3.5 some relatively high scores: position (11) was scored at 64%, fear/anxiety felt by team members (10) was at 53%, extrinsic incentives (9) and controlling (12) were both scored at 44%. This might on the surface seem concerning, but again, if we consider the context and understand what the team leader was trying to achieve, these scores make sense.

This case study provides a very good example of the distinction between formal and informal influence (authority) that we discussed in Chapter 1. Formal influence is given by the organisation to the team leader. We can see this in the team leader's ability to offer extrinsic incentives (9), to use disciplinary processes that created a degree of fear or anxiety (10), to use position or rank (11) as a form of influence, and finally to be directive and tell team members what is expected of them in terms of controlling (12). In this case study, the team leader was using the formal forms of influence given to him by the organisation in an attempt to transform the performance of the team.

Whilst there are some indications from his scores that the team leader could work through his expert and reward attributes to transform his team, as we have noted earlier, these take time to be recognised by team members. We also know from the context that there were difficult, resistant, and poor-performing individual team members in the team. To transform the team and its performance, the team leader had therefore to draw on their transactional influences most strongly during their early period in the role, i.e., the influences from extrinsic incentives, fear/anxiety, position/rank, and controlling.

It is interesting that using these formal forms of influence did not have a negative effect on other areas of the leader's leadership profile. Perhaps the more conscientious team members **wanted him** to use formal means and his rank or position to control, discipline, and use other incentives to 'correct' the poor performers in their team. Poor performers often 'let down' others in a team and so the team **expected** the team leader to act – and do so decisively.

CONCLUSIONS AND INSIGHTS

It was only through the LPA diagnostic instrument that the pattern described in Figure 3.5 emerged. It was a revelation to the team leader in their feedback session and gave them added confidence for the path they were engaged on. In such cases, once the team and its performance had been transformed the team leader will then have less need to use their formal forms of influence, so we would expect the perceptions and scores here to drop back over time. However, the case illustrates well, the importance of transactional forms of influence in the overall profile of a leader. Not only is this type of influence available, if necessary, but in many cases the team members expect it to be drawn on by the team leader, and failure to do so would undermine their 'acceptance' of their influence as leaders.

CASE STUDY 3.6: A CASE OF FAILED 'LEADERSHIP' BUT BUSINESS SUCCESS. THIS IS NOT A REAL CASE STUDY BUT CONSTRUCTED WITH HINDSIGHT

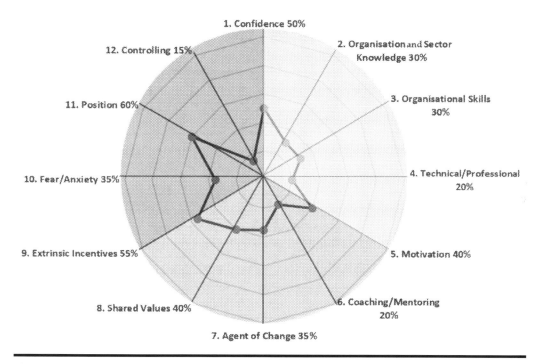

Figure 3.6   A case of failed 'leadership' but business success

INTRODUCTION

The failed leadership case below would not have happened if Geoff, the co-author of this book, had had the LPA available at the time, which was 30 years ago. He remained in contact with the team members for many years after he left the role, so, he could, retrospectively, apply the 12 forms of influence based on their helpful criticism and reflections much later. So, Figure 3.6 is an estimate, a critical self-evaluation. At the time, he tended to blame them for resisting the changes he was trying to bring in. From the work he has done in developing both ETL and the LPA, he now sees that it was **his** lack of awareness that was the main cause of his failure to be 'willingly and enthusiastically accepted' as a team leader by his team during the first 18 months in the role.

Background

Geoff took over the management of a small department in a university that carried out basic management training. The department had a loss-making income of £650,000 at the time. He had previously been employed as a lecturer in an academic department, in another part of the University.

This training department consisted of experienced management trainers. Geoff was appointed as he believed the future for the department was linking management training with qualifications. He also believed that the future of management education was more about distance learning with interactive workshops as opposed to lectures. He was reminded of the comment that 'the notes of the lecturer passed to the notes of the students without passing through the minds of either!' So, his plan was that instead of students from large organisations going to the university, on day release, or evening classes, the department would run in-company programmes. Every two months there would be in-company two-day workshops linked to marked assignments and projects.

Taking education out of colleges and universities was a relatively new idea in those days. Typical courses would be certificate in management studies (CMS), diploma in management studies (DMS), and even master's in business administration (MBA). At that time, only Polytechnics and Universities could offer qualifications, and this was going to be Geoff's department's unique selling point (USP) against competitors offering just management training that did not lead to qualifications.

Geoff presented his vision for the future to the department staff a couple of months before he took over. By the time he took over at least three experienced management trainers had already left, basically to set up their own management training companies not linked to qualifications, taking with them previous university clients.

The next 18 months caused considerable stress and anxiety for those that remained. Geoff was told by his team that the only person who didn't understand what was going on was himself. Some individuals even complained to the principal of the University, as they were worried about their future under his 'team leadership'. However, after 18 months, more staff were being recruited and the turnover was moving towards £2m. The department had eventually become very profitable, and the staff were also much more content.

INTERPRETING THE CASE USING THE ETL AND LPA

If we now look, with the benefit of hindsight, at the context and the 12 forms of influence linked to team leadership, or the lack of it, we can see why Geoff might have had such a struggle to get the team to 'accept his influence willingly and enthusiastically'. Of course, the analysis below can only be seen as tentative, we have not been able to ask the team members to complete their LPAs as they would have done at the time of the original events. However, let us look at each area of influence based on what we do know.

TRANSACTIONAL (FORMAL FORMS OF INFLUENCE)

Like Case Study 3.5, Geoff initially had to rely on transactional forms of influence. He was head of department (rank), so he could push through the new strategy and vision even if staff resisted. In addition, the principal of the University supported him and his strategy (another form of position influence). Geoff therefore had two forms of position influence (11).

There were also extrinsic incentives available to him (9), as the staff were expected to work a full year with no long academic holidays. In compensation, all the staff were put on higher salaries and had company cars – as nearly all their work was outside the university. But as we have seen in previous cases studies, relying on transactional influence does not equate to team leadership.

EXPERT (INFORMAL FORMS OF INFLUENCE)

When it came to organisation and sector knowledge (2), Geoff felt that he had the knowledge about what client organisations wanted (i.e., a more flexible approach to management education and training), but he failed to convince team members of his expertise here or the accuracy of his analysis. He just assumed staff shared his vision and analysis. Geoff also failed to effectively communicate the changing needs of industry and commerce in terms of management education. So, in the eyes of his team, he appeared to lack organisation and sector knowledge, although this perception was largely due to poor communication on his part.

Geoff was also preoccupied with programme development and selling his new ideas to companies rather than keeping on top of organising and administration (3). As he failed to deal with administration and HR issues quickly, so in the eyes of team members he was viewed as lacking a degree of managerial competence.

One of his greatest failings though, in the eyes of team members, was his lack of technical or professional expertise (4). In team members' eyes, Geoff was merely an academic who had no knowledge of the world of management training, which was the expertise of the team.

SOCIAL AND EMOTIONAL REWARD (INFORMAL INFLUENCE)

Team members were motivated when it came to management training, but not motivated to convert such programmes to academic programmes. In effect, Geoff's strategy weakened their motivation (5) as they were not interested in the new strategy. Geoff was so focused on the USP and the future that he failed to reassure team members that management training, not linked to qualifications, would continue, if there was still demand for them.

Because Geoff was perceived to have very little knowledge about training, the team members did not look to him for their own coaching, mentoring, training, or development (6). Team members were not interested in learning from him; in their eyes, he had very little knowledge and experience that they valued.

Geoff was clearly an agent of change (7), but in the eyes of team members such changes had little or no benefit for them. When he took on the role of head of department, he was told to make money for the university or close the department down. He did not believe it was sensible to mention the possibility of closure to his team, so, perhaps rightly, kept this information to himself.

Finally, Geoff and the team, over most of the first 18 months of his appointment, did not share the same vision and values (8). They saw their department becoming another academic department, whilst he saw management education moving out of the universities and being more client company and user-friendly.

CONCLUSIONS AND INSIGHTS

It is now, over 30 years later, that Geoff fully understands why he struggled to lead a team of very able and interesting professional people. He spent a very stressful 18 months trying to 'manage the team' because he had no real knowledge about what 'team leadership' really entailed. It is only now, looking back, that he understands that the business success he and his team achieved was down to having the right strategy at the right time, but not down to his team leadership. If Geoff had been aware of the 12 forms of influence, when he took over the team, then he is quite clear that progress would have been much quicker. Above all that change of strategy would not have generated conflict, frustration, aggression, anxiety, and the loss of very able team members.

Chapter Summary

The case studies we have included in this chapter just show a sketch of what information is generated by the LPA. The LPA gives us detailed insight into each of the 12 forms of influence so we can see why the scores are high or low, particularly when those giving the feedback look closer at the five elements behind each of the 12 forms of influence.

This detail can be used by anyone giving feedback whether as a management consultant, a trainer, a coach, an appraiser, or indeed the team leader reviewing the data themselves. In the next chapter, we will look at the range of potential applications of this model in organisations.

Chapter 4

Features, Benefits, and Practical Application of ETL and the LPA

As demonstrated by the case studies in the previous chapter, our experience of working with Emergent Team Leadership (ETL) and Leadership Pathway Audit (LPA) has highlighted that …

- **It's easily understood and relatable**: ETL/LPA arrives at descriptions that team leaders can relate to; the 12 key forms of influence are understood by the team leader whose profile is being reviewed as well as by team members.
- **It provides explanations**: ETL/LPA can arrive at explanations because we have an 'operational definition of team leadership'. Team leadership exists as an emergent social property which can be directly or indirectly observed from team members' perceptions. See chapter 5.
- **Shows leaders the path to develop leadership**: ETL/LPA defines team leadership clearly and can be practically applied to help team leaders develop *leadership.* Books and articles, seemingly without exception, either have no operational definition of leadership or define leadership in such a broad way that it cannot be used to explain, describe, or make forecasts. ETL/LPA creates a clear and direct pathway for leaders developing themselves and getting the team to succeed.
- **It connects with performance realities**: ETL/LPA strengthens the link between the team leader, their team, and organisational

DOI: 10.4324/9781003475569-4

performance, i.e., team productivity, staff retention, absence, staff survey results, stress, and anxiety.

- **Provides profiles unique to the leader**: ETL/LPA defines a bespoke profile for every leader rather than forcing them into existing groups of personality types or models of required behaviour.
- **Focuses on team members' perceptions**: ETL/LPA is not leader-centric but instead suggests a key active role and inclusion for team members in the emergence of 'leadership'.
- **Is flexible and adaptable over time**: ETL/LPA does not suggest a static view of a leader – it highlights that perceptions change over time and as a role changes. Leaders can measure themselves and their progress over time such that ETL/LPA provides the basis for lifelong learning and development.
- **Deals with realities not ideals**: ETL/LPA is not focused on creating idealistic (and unrealistic) leaders. Books and articles also tend to concentrate on what leadership ***ought*** to be, based on value judgement and assumptions. ETL/LPA concentrates on what team leadership ***is*** and how it emerges in organisations; it is neutral and value-free.

LPA Provides a Lot of Data

The LPA has the added advantage of providing information about the team. It is informative about how the team is thinking and perceiving. Agreement and disagreement within the team can be seen when you examine and compare the data from each individual respondent to the audit. Team members have different perceptions, and this will be shown in the range of results, even for the same type of influence. The amount of data generated can also be analysed from several perspectives. Teams may be cohesive or less cohesive and this can be identified and is helpful to recognise.

Face Validity

ETL is simple to understand, recognised as relevant by leaders themselves, and has practical outcomes. It therefore has *face validity*, relevance, and impact. See testimonials in the last chapter.

The Potential Benefits for the Organisation of ETL

Based on our research and work to date, we can also see multiple potential benefits for organisation in applying ETL/LPA.

- **Development needs**: ETL/LPA can define future development needs for both teams and organisations if applied widely.
- **Culture change**: ETL/LPA enables an organisation to track culture change over time. This can be done even as organisations and markets change. The culture of an organisation, whether 'good' or 'bad', is transmitted through teams and through their team leaders. Team are the vehicles through which change happens. The organisation can therefore use ETL/LPA as an instrument of culture reinforcement or culture change.
- **Well-being**: ETL/LPA enables an organisation to continually monitor the relationship between teams and their team leaders. This relationship has a direct link to team performance and employee well-being.
- **Leadership data**: ETL/LPA can deliver big data across an organisation, providing analytics that looks at the reality of leadership by level, role, age, characteristics, specialisation, or any other comparison – so providing an evolving view of *leadership* that organisations need and want to understand.

As we will see later in this chapter, ETL/LPA can also be applied in many different processes and contexts within organisations, e.g., team leadership coaching, training, appraising, selecting, and improving employee well-being.

The Particular Benefit for Individual Leaders from Understanding Their ETL and LPA Profile

Besides the benefits for organisations, the primary benefits are apparent for team leaders themselves.

- **Gives genuine insight into their team leadership**: Leadership, as described by ETL and the LPA, is what leaders themselves are looking for, i.e., a team that works with them and supports them (see testimonials at the end of the book). The LPA profile outlines what the team is looking for from their leader.

- **Tracking personal development and progress**: The profile is not about the leader's fixed personality but about the team's perceptions – and those perceptions can be changed. The LPA profile itself is also a product that can be continually referred to and this then enables leaders to have a regular audit and measure changes and improvements over time and as the role changes.
- **It is realistic and practical**: The LPA profile does not focus on identifying what is good or bad – it focuses on what exists. The profile is built on science and evidence, not a vague concept or managerial discussion.
- **It is targeted and specific**: The LPA profile itself provides hundreds of data points for a team leader or a coach to consider. The profile will define and specify future development needs for individuals rather than suggesting generic 'leadership training'.
- **It supports performance and well-being**: Once a team leader understands how they are perceived and to what extent they are perceived as displaying 'leadership', the team and team leader will be under less stress. The leader will also be more confident in being able to introduce innovation, improvement, and change with less team resistance.
- **Acts as a warning to complacency**: ETL and the LPA indicate that the team leader must continually work on their leadership; team perceptions can and will change. Team leadership may not exist on a knife's edge, but conditions are always changing. There is no room for complacency.

POTENTIAL APPLICATIONS OF ETL/LPA IN ORGANISATIONS

We will explore below the practical use of ETL and LPA in areas such as setting SMART objectives, coaching, performance reviews, training, promotions, and culture change.

ETL Satisfies SMART Criteria

All managers are told that any organisational objectives, they set in performance reviews, in coaching, or in training, should be SMART, meaning specific, measurable, achievable, relevant (realistic), and time bound. ETL and the LPA fulfil these requirements. This then strengthens their value when applied in the contexts of coaching, appraisals, training, and promotion as we will show later.

- **Specific**. The approach is specific in that it refers to the leadership found in teams and no other social situation. It is specific in that it concentrates on the perception of team members. It is specific in that it concentrates on 12 forms of perceived influence.
- **Measurable**. Using the LPA, we can measure the degree to which team members perceive their team leader in terms of three broad forms of influence. We can repeat the LPA to measure the degree to which team members' perceptions have changed, after team leader training or coaching.
- **Achievable**. Team leaders can improve the way they communicate and what they communicate after training. Team leadership is not dependent on the team leader's personality which is often seen as fixed. The basis of ETL is practical steps or a *pathway* team leaders can take to maintain or improve their profile.
- **Relevant (or realistic)**. Our case study field research has found that team leaders desire a situation where team members willingly and enthusiastically accept them. Such an outcome they see as relevant, and it has an impact on how they approach and lead their team. Many team leaders go on leadership courses hoping that they will be helped to create a situation where team members work with them and support them. Anecdotally, we have found that team leaders, and prospective team leaders, have been disappointed about the outcomes arising from leadership courses they have attended. Such courses often concentrate on the team leader's role and responsibilities and the outcomes expected of them, but do not cover **how to achieve** such outcomes through the team itself!
- **Time Bound**. ETL is based on the LPA diagnostic tool. It only takes team members about ten minutes to complete. As soon as all team members have completed the LPA then the team leader should receive feedback promptly – days, not months later. This promptness of feedback is important as the impact of the report and feedback is diminished if the feedback is slow – the team leader can always excuse the feedback by saying that things have changed since then. The perception of team members can be retested after coaching or training to identify any improvement. However, changing the team members' perception does not happen overnight, it is more realistic to retest after four to six months.

ETL as a Coaching Tool

The aim of a coach is to ask questions and probe, more than just supplying answers. Questioning is much more effective than just delivering solutions. ETL and the LPA provide the coach with a multitude of questions, and the LPA profile particularly is a most fruitful area for exploration. ETL is therefore a perfect fit for the coaching process.

The simplest model to adopt in coaching, and easiest to understand, is the GROW model. This stands for goal, reality, options, and way ahead (Alexander, 2010; Whitmore, 1992).

1. **Goal**: The coach and client set the context for the interaction. What does the client want from the process? What are the objectives of the leadership coaching process?
   - From our experience, the key desire for team leaders is to have a team that willingly and enthusiastically accept them, which is the very aim of ETL and the LPA.
   - There might, though, be several other 'goals' when it comes to leadership coaching. For example, the client might want a better relationship with the team, they might want to introduce innovation, improvement, and change with the minimum of resistance, or they might simply want to improve team performance. If they find leading their team stressful then their goal might be to interact with their team in a less stressful manner. The leader might therefore want to know how their team perceive them so that they can adjust that perception. Above all, their central goal will be to create a situation of *leadership*, i.e., where their team see them as displaying team leadership as we have defined it.
2. **Reality**: The second step in the coaching process is to look at the current situation and identify where the leader is now compared to where they want to be. Are the goals discussed above realistic? Above all what is the team's perception?
   - This can be accurately measured by the LPA. The audit gives the team leader and the coach a realistic indication of where the team leader is now when it comes to the 12 forms of influence. These can be all broken down into even more focused topics that the coach can use to generate relevant questions. LPA is an immensely powerful diagnostic tool that gives the leader an accurate picture of how team members perceive them, i.e., the current reality.

3. **Options**: What are the options or opportunities for the team leader to change their team members' perceptions?

   – In coaching, it is often difficult to know where to start but our four headings under expert forms of influence, four headings under reward forms of influence, and four headings under transactional forms provide a good range of options for this. In some organisational cultures, team members may expect position, controlling, fear, and extrinsic incentives to be normal and not see them as negative in any way.

   – Either way, in a coaching session, you would decide which areas are likely to be the most promising 'options' for meeting your defined 'goals'.

4. **Way ahead**: At the end of each coaching session, there should be a clear action plan.

   – There may be several ways ahead the team leader can create (their own) action plan drawing on their LPA audit. As we have indicated already, just changing their own behaviour is unlikely to change the team members' perceptions, especially in the short term. If the team leader wants to change their team members' perceptions, he or she could discuss their action plans with their team.

   – One of the key points about our definition of leadership and how it relates to the 12 headings is that, in an agreed time later, the team can complete another LPA. Any change in perceptions and its link to team leadership can then be seen. The desired changes here should help shape the way ahead in the action plan.

ETL Within Team Leaders' Performance Reviews or Appraisals

There is more to an appraisal process than merely a discussion of team leadership, but as team leadership has an impact on team performance, it is an especially important discussion point and may also lead to the identification of training and coaching needs.

Ideally, the appraiser needs to be trained to use the LPA and to give feedback on it and the appraisee's team, of course, would need to have already completed an LPA. Words such as strengths, weaknesses, good, bad, wrong, right, improve, ought, etc. should then be avoided in the discussions.

High scores for expert or reward (informal) influence can be 'built on'. The team leader could be encouraged to consider how to change their team's perceptions where they have been given low scores for expert or reward influence or at least discuss them with the appraiser. Transactional scores should be discussed with reference to their own specific context including the culture of the organisation – and indeed the whole profile should always be analysed in the specific organisational context.

Similarly, appraisers should concentrate on the whole profile, not just concentrate on one or two of the 12 forms of influence. Different team leaders may have different profiles, but those different profiles could still indicate the existence or not of team leadership. Appraisers should therefore put the resulting profile in context by considering issues such as: What is the organisations culture? What issues confront the organisation at this moment in time that might have an impact on the team members' perceptions? What local issues does the team leader need to deal with right now?

When comparing team leaders, it is the whole profile that is important. It would, however, be important to see if those with a clearer perceived profile of *leadership* have more 'productive' teams than those with a less clear or weaker perception of team leadership. See Chapter 5.

It is though important to recognise that a team leader who is not perceived by team members as displaying team leadership may still be 'effective', in the sense of delivering results. The appraiser should not therefore criticise their profile results, but instead, adopt a coaching style to help the team leader. Having a team that accepts the leader's influence 'willingly and enthusiastically' will after all have advantages for both the team leader, the team, and the organisation.

ETL and Leadership Training for Established Team Leaders

ETL and the LPA can be used in a training situation where there may be several team leaders in a leadership training workshop. Training can be delivered through segments, each with a different emphasis. The training programme should have the minimum of trainer input and the maximum of experiential learning. In advance of the training workshop, team profiles should have been completed, but the outcomes should not be delivered to those individuals in the workshop until an appropriate time. Needless to say, the LPA report only goes to individuals to look at. In the main session, the trainer should discuss general principles and not about individual profiles. Part of the programme would be about the practical steps team leaders can take to influence team member perceptions with reference to all three team members' perceptions of expert, reward, and transactional.

ETL and Leadership Training for New Team Leaders or Those About to Become Team Leaders

We suggest that the trainer starts off with a plenary discussion about how, from the trainee's experience, they have evaluated their own team leaders in the past, leading into small group discussions and presentations based on their experiences. The trainer can then highlight how their new team will judge them in a similar way to how they have judged other team leaders.

The trainer should then introduce the team to ETL and the LPA and discuss how their own perceptions of leaders they have worked with relate to the two approaches.

The 12 forms of influence can then be discussed from a practical point of view and the differences between formal and informal influence are highlighted. The aim here will be to stress that informal influence has huge advantages for team leadership. It will be helpful to then mention that their new team will be completing the LPA in a few months' time, possibly four to six months. This advanced warning will concentrate on the learning process.

LPA in Promotion or Job Applications

Many of our team leaders, having received the LPA report, not only keep it to remind themselves of the basis for team leadership but also as a 'reference' whenever, and if ever, they apply for other roles or seek promotion.

Modern selection processes assess jobs and candidates against a list of 'competences' in the selection process. These competences associated with the role tend to include:

■ Professional and technical competences
■ System and procedure competences
■ Intrapersonal and team competences

In many ways, all three competences are being evaluated by team members when it comes to team leadership, but the most relevant one is 'team competences' as we convert that to team leadership. In individual team leader can show the degree to which his or her present team perceive them in terms of leadership. That is the degree to which team members willingly and enthusiastically accept them as their leader.

ETL Role in Team Leadership Culture

Our experience as team members, team leaders, and coaches and trainers suggests that team leaders may well emulate the team leader above them. If they have experience of a team leader who influences through social and emotional rewards, then they might well do the same with their team. The reverse may also be true. One of the authors trained team leaders in conducting performance reviews and some team leaders commented, 'why should I conduct performance reviews with my staff when my boss never bothers to conduct a performance review with me?'

Improved team leadership as described by ETL may well cascade down the organisation and improve the whole organisations team leadership culture.

Important Things to Consider in the Application of ETL

Keeping the LPA Focused Just on Team Members

The team leader should not complete their own audit, LPA, – as is common in 360-degree surveys. There are two main reasons for this:

1. Very few team leaders have a real understanding of themselves and how they come across.
2. The team view is nearly always different from the team leader's own view of themselves, and this may create 'cognitive dissonance' (first described by Festinger in 1957). Cognitive dissonance occurs when two ideas clash, which may lead to the team's perception being rejected or watered down by their team leader. As Fritz Heider (1958) pointed out, in interpersonal relationships, people seek a balance of ideas. So, if the leader judged themselves one way and saw that the team's judgement

was different, the leader would seek to restore balance, perhaps by treating the team's judgement as somehow less valid, and in this way restoring balance with their own judgement. What is important and relevant is the team's *perception* not their leader's own perception of themselves.

In our field study research, we also found that some team leaders wanted to include colleagues and not just team members in the audit. This again often happened in organisations that had a 360-degree appraisal system. However, the LPA is designed for team members only, not other stakeholders; it is only the team members' perception of the leader's influence profile that is being measured. Other stakeholders do not evaluate the team leader in the same way, in terms of influence, but use other criteria.

Comparing Team Leader Profiles

Because different team leaders have different personalities and have teams with different experiences, it would be wrong to 'exactly' compare one team leader with the next. If team leader A scores 65% for confidence and team leader B scores 75%, this is not as important as the whole profile. From the team members' perspective, the leaders may have different 'profiles' but could still be seen as providing 'leadership' in our definition.

LPA and New Leaders

As we saw from a case study in Chapter 3, the LPA is likely to indicate that the relationship between a new leader and their team will be based disproportionally on *Transactional* forms of influence because Expert and Reward perceptions take time to be recognised or felt. An LPA conducted after a team leader has been in the role for six months or more provides a better indication of that leader's profile once they and their team are in a more settled state.

It may though still be very useful for very new team leaders to be introduced to ETL and shown what they need to do to move from merely *managing* their team to *leadership*. However, at some stage, they need to find out their team's perception of them as a team leader.

Why the LPA Might Not Indicate Team Leadership

Our approach is scientific, so we do not use terms like good, bad, success, failure, etc. As team leadership is an 'emergent social property', it has either emerged, is emerging, or has yet to emerge. Below are several reasons why team leadership may not appear to have emerged in their LPA profile.

- **A new leader**: The team leader is new to the role, new to the team, and the only influence they have is transactional, such as position and job title.

- **If values/goals of the team are different from those of the leader**: One of the authors worked with a team who were totally opposed (unlike their team leader), to efficiency and effectiveness. The team's view then was that being more efficient/effective would lead to senior management reducing the size of the team and cutting staff (this is not an unrealistic assumption!).

- **If the team leader lacks awareness**: When a leader is unaware of the perception of their team members when it comes to his or her profile, such team leaders might be concentrating on the type of profile or influence they **think** would impress team members when in fact team members have different expectations. As such, the team leaders and the team's definition of team leadership and their expectations may be quite different. In some cases, the team leader may try to deliver what they think their senior managers consider to be team leadership – for example, a more controlling style or one based on fear/anxiety.

- **If the context is driving the leader's actions**: The team leader might have to impose decisions that team members disagree with or are hostile to – such as redundancies or new ways of working, which they do not understand and may feel threatened by. Similarly, there may be situations where a team leader is taking over a difficult or hostile team, or where there is poor team cohesion, poor team support, or lack of training. In such situations, the team leader will have to work hard to create a suitable context to enable a perception of team leadership to emerge. The leader may have to work hard to move the situation into leadership. His or her key task is to try to change team members' perceptions though, as much as the context.

■ **If the leader is a poor communicator**: Where the team leader does not communicate information to team members that indicates any form of expertise, i.e., expert influence. They should not be surprised if the team does not view them positively on a range of forms of influence.

■ **If the leader appears disinterested in their team**: The leader may not be seen to be interested in developing team members (training, coaching, and mentoring), or encouraging their motivation as a social and emotional reward. Perhaps they are making the assumptions that team members are only motivated by money? The power of the LPA is that it identifies any mismatch between the team leader and their team members' expectations.

■ **If the leader appears not to value their team**: Here, the team leader may take success for granted and does not recognise that achieving targets or exceeding targets is an opportunity for individual and team recognition, i.e., reward influence.

■ **If leaders or team members hold prejudices**: Prejudices based on gender and ethnicity may exist that distort team members' perceptions, especially when it comes to shared work values. Team members might be prejudging the team leader or the team leader prejudging the team members. An example is when a team leader treats female team members in a manner that might best be described in terms of misogyny. Also, in some cultures, male team members may not perceive a female team leader as having informal influence based on expertise or socio-emotional rewards. Even in western cultures, female team leaders may have to work much harder to be accepted, willingly and enthusiastically by male team members, especially in male-dominated organisations and industries.

■ **If the leader is not suited to the role**: For whatever reason, the team leader may be unsuited to the role of team leadership. One of the authors was helping the development of a small company. The male owner was highly skilled in new technologies; he had developed the right products at the right time and his business was growing. Through working with the LPA, he came to recognise that he had transactional authority, being the owner, and he also had technical and professional skills. However, he recognised his limitations when it came to getting the team of 15 to 'enthusiastically' accept him. Once he recognised this through his LPA profile, he appointed a managing director who could meet the expectations and perceptions desired by the team to establish team *leadership*, whilst his own role then became one of technical director.

Changing the Perceptions of Team Members

Perceptions of Leadership Are Not Constant

Because ETL arrives at a relevant profile, based on team members' perceptions, it is a measure at one or more moments in time, which has the advantage that the perception, and thus the leader's profile, can be changed.

In some circumstances, the team perception can be altered by outside factors such as an organisation downsizing, or the team leader having to impose decisions without question, often dictated by external events. ETL is thus a *contingency* model of leadership. The profile should always be looked at in its *social context*; it is, after all, an emergent social property!

Leadership Is Contextual: Moving In and Out of Leadership

If a team leader, perceived as displaying 'leadership' by team members, is forced to impose policies that the team totally or partially oppose – policies that perhaps benefit the organisation in some way but are not perceived as such by team members – then a perception of their *leadership* may disappear. The team leader may have to accept this but may return to a position of perceived leadership once the policies have been introduced. Moving in and out of *perceived leadership* is not good or bad; it is organisational life!

Effective Communication Is Essential for Changing Perceptions

The Chartered Management Institute (CMI), United Kingdom, research report (2023), mentioned at the start of the book, found that when employees rated their line manager as ineffective there were negative consequences from this in terms of team performance and labour turnover. ETL locates precisely where, if anywhere, the team leader is **not** seen as delivering the leadership team members need. This is in the eyes of team members so the team leader can focus on what to do, based on the 12 key forms of influence. By taking practical steps through more effective communication, the team leader can improve his or her image in the eyes of team members.

How ETL Can Reduce Stress, Anxiety, and Promote Employee Well-Being

Many things that cause stress and anxiety at work are the result of a poor relationship between team members and team leaders – as we saw in the CMI survey mentioned at the beginning of Chapter 1. The LPA identifies the in-depth relationship between team members and the team leader and can locate the possible causes of stress, anxiety, frustration, and conflict. For example, stress and anxiety might be found in high transactional perceptions, low expert perceptions, or low reward perceptions.

Often team members who are stressed are given time off for counselling or recovery because HR departments may not realise that the stress is caused by the team leader. Often the team leader themselves has no idea about the effect they are having, as it is not intentional. One team member in our research commented that their leader was a pleasant enough person but "a nightmare to work with".

Stress and anxiety often result in absenteeism, unnecessary labour turnover, and poor performance. We also note that if team members do not 'willingly and enthusiastically accept their leader' then the team leader themselves may well also suffer from stress and anxiety.

We have seen in our research and case studies though that the existence of a *leadership* profile, however, means that the leader is under less stress and so are the team members. Leading others is not an easy process, but the existence of *leadership* where 'team members willingly and enthusiastically accept the leader' by definition is linked to a less stressful interaction.

Bernard Bass (1999a, 1999b: pp. 11–12) also commented "… we know from research about how transformational leadership enhances commitment, involvement, loyalty, and performance of followers; how transactional leadership may induce more stress; how transformational leadership helps deal with stress amongst followers". Implicit in the term 'transformational leadership', used by Bass, are things such as empathy, being alert to individual's needs, providing learning opportunities, intellectual stimulations, etc. Our explanation of leadership includes these elements, although they are not necessarily *transformational*, which is a term used as a value judgment by Bass. Also, as we have said before, terms such as 'followers' are far from helpful.

Conclusion

Our approach to team leadership stresses the importance of the team members' perceptions, which can be measured. This has opened a multitude of advantages for team leaders, coaches, trainers, consultants, and appraisers. The strength of ETL can be seen in its very wide application from culture change to employee well-being. By looking at team leadership with a different emphasis it has created considerable insight, far more than we ever imagined when we first created ETL.

Chapter 5

The Building Blocks of Emergent Team Leadership Are Derived from Basic Social Science

We start off this chapter by looking at our definition of leadership as an emergent social property, our approach is team-centric, not leader-centric. We then move on to describe what an explanation is in science and the social sciences, operational definitions, concepts as scaffolds, myths, and value judgement, forecasts as opposed to predictions, and finally, the link between leadership and business success.

Our Definition of Leadership as an Emergent Social Property

As we have seen earlier, there is a dubious and often repeated claim in the leadership literature that team leadership is some 'property' of the team leader or manager, but there is no empirical evidence for this. Challenging this traditional perspective, Haslam et al. (2011) refer to E. P. Hollander (1995) and noted how he (Hollander) "…points, amongst other things, to the role that group plays in validating and empowering the leader and to the importance of followers in the leadership process" (2011: p. 63).

In our book and model, we do not refer to 'followers' because generally team members do not see themselves as *followers*, it is often the thoughtless

 DOI: 10.4324/9781003475569-5

use of language which lets down any objective discussion in science or in our case the discussion of leadership. We therefore looked instead at team leadership as a **perception** in the minds of team members. When we did so, we found that such an approach will enable us to describe, explain, and make forecasts. Whilst there may not be common characteristics amongst team leaders when it comes to team leadership, through our research, we did find many common characteristics when it comes to the perception of team members, based on their expectations and experience around their idea of team leader **influence**.

In this book, you will see that our perspective is that leadership is **socially constructed.** What that means is that what some people see as 'good' leadership (e.g., seeking the ideas of team members before making decisions) in one context might be viewed as 'weak' leadership in another (e.g., where the leader is supposed to be decisive and know all the right answers themselves). How leadership is perceived depends on the specific social environment, organisational culture, and/or societal culture. It is therefore dangerous to assume that what works in one context will work equally well in another.

Therefore, team leadership cannot be taken out of its social context – it is an 'emergent social property' rather than a property of the team leader or manager. As leadership is socially constructed, it is influenced by society and the culture of the organisation. We have therefore confined ourselves to leadership of 'teams' and have also then identified the necessary conditions for leadership to emerge in such teams.

From this, ETL has an operational definition, not based on the leader, but based on the perception of team members. ETL also has a diagnostic tool, the LPA, which provides the means for measurement of leadership as it emerges in any situation and context.

Explanations (Explaining How Leadership Emerges in Teams)

In science, an explanation is a 'list of the necessary conditions which are jointly sufficient for an event', an event such as the emergence of team leadership. We provide those necessary conditions which are jointly sufficient when team members perceive their leader as providing them with social and emotional rewards. But social and emotional rewards were also dependent on how team members perceived their leader as having managerial expertise or credibility.

In some organisational cultures, transactional forms of influence/authority such as position or rank might also be important in explaining what is seen as significant in team members' perceptions.

In this book, we refer to two types of explanation. One is based on basic science, and the other one, used in the social sciences, arrives at 'meaningfully adequate' explanations. They are interdependent.

Scientific Explanations

Scientific explanations tend to show a link or correlation between events. We can test and retest to show links, sometimes in lay terms called causes. Later in this book, we discuss Goleman's link between business success and the business leader having 'emotional intelligence'. This is a correlation, not an explanation; in fact, later we will show that ETL provides the missing explanation, a 'meaningfully adequate explanation'.

Meaningfully Adequate Explanations

We understand, from our own experience and expectations, why people behave in a certain way under certain social conditions. When it comes to understanding why team members willingly and enthusiastically accept their leader's formal and informal influence, we can always ask them and use our own experience to come up with a plausible explanation.

When it comes to team leadership, team members are more willing to accept their leader's influence if the leader is perceived as having managerial competence or expertise. Also, if the relationship between the leader and the team is socio-emotionally rewarding for team members then the leader's influence is more likely to be enthusiastically accepted.

Our explanation for the emergence of leadership in teams is meaningfully adequate. If we look at the four social and emotional rewards, we are not saying that if one of them was missing there would be no team leadership as we defined it, but the leadership *pathway* might be weakened.

The German sociologist Max Weber (1864–1920) used the term 'verstehen' or 'intuitive understanding' in describing sociological explanations. Sociology as a science aims at an interpretative understanding of social actions to gain an explanation of its causes, its courses, and its effect. We use the term meaningfully adequate explanations; we understand the motives or the reasons behind events because we live in that society. A scientist might discover that more ice cream is consumed in Western Europe in the summer, but we have a meaningfully adequate explanation of why.

To understand this, consider the following situation …

- Team leader Green believes he or is displaying *leadership,* of their team, but their team does not perceive them as displaying *leadership.* Leader Brown does not believe he or she is displaying team leadership, of their team, but their team does perceive them as displaying leadership. It is the second example where we would say that leadership exists – because it exists in the minds of the team members. They are the only judges that matter!
- If team leadership is based on the expectations and experience of team members then a team leader who has been on a leadership training/ coaching programme and who tries to change their behaviour will often end up returning to their old style, pushed, and persuaded by the expectations of team members. This seems to us to be very common. A team leader changing their behaviour does not automatically mean that their team members will change their perceptions.
- If, however, the team leader realises that team leadership is based on team members' perception, they might explain to team members **why** they are changing their behaviour so that team members perceive that behaviour in a different way. It is not the behaviour that is important but how that behaviour is **perceived**.

By explaining events with reference to how individuals think and feel we, as fellow human beings, arrive at explanations. In this way, we have 'meaningfully adequate' explanations.

In the natural sciences, an explanation is a list of the necessary conditions which are **jointly sufficient** for an event. Under laboratory conditions, variables can be taken away or added to show they are necessary. In the social sciences, this is seldom possible, especially with large social events. However, what we can do is ask ourselves: How we would react if one of the conditions were removed? How would we react if we felt our team leader had different values from us? How would we react if the team leader was uninterested in our work and development? Such questions lead to explanations which are meaningfully adequate.

In the social science of economics, meaningfully adequate explanations are frequently used. If the price of a non-essential item goes up, then less will be sold. We do not need a statistician or researcher to explain why this happens – we have all purchased items and so intuitively know why. If, on the other hand, the price falls then more will be sold. However, we are also aware, that if a high-status non-essential item falls in price, then less might be sold. The best example is perfume: if the price of some perfume product is reduced and you can purchase it at the local petrol station, then sales will go down. We meaningfully understand why: those people wearing it will lose status – they are buying cheaper scent.

Operational Definitions

Operational definitions are designed to help us arrive at possible descriptions, explanations, and forecasts (predictions in the natural sciences). Concepts such as team leadership need to be defined. The lack of progress in the study of leadership is that no one seems to have arrived at an operational definition but instead relied on vague implications about what the concept might mean, sometimes even leaving the concept open-ended as in everyday use.

Trainers and coaches in effect are saying "You desire team leadership, and we can train you in team leadership – but we are not going to tell you what team leadership is!"

Peter Fuda (2013: p. X) commented

> I had become more and more frustrated with the literature. In my reading of both academic and practitioner-oriented texts, I struggled with a long list of qualities and attributes that defined 'effective' leadership, and with the heroic persona that was often attributed to the person sitting atop the organisational hierarchy - they espoused largely noble attributes like vision, courage, and integrity. The problem was that, after so many years of working closely with CEOs and senior executives around the world, I have never met the superhero leader described in much of what I read.

You can have any definition of team leadership you like, but does it lead to explanations? The key challenge to overcome is: Does your definition help to answer the questions you are asking?

Most authors seem to accept the word 'leadership' without any attempt to define it – it is an everyday word and different people give it different meanings. But everyday words are inadequate in trying to explain events.

For example, Jeffrey Pfeffer, an influential writer on management and leadership in organisations, suggests in a recent text (2016: p. 95) that "leadership" is the ability "to get things done". Such an approach is not really a definition and would be useless for research purposes.

In the United States, there has been a tendency to 'define' leadership in terms of business success, this too is a limited perspective, vague and full of value judgements. Kotter (1988: p. 5) footnotes "Leadership is.... The process of moving a group (or groups) in some direction through mostly non-coercive means. Effective leadership is.... Leadership that produces movement in the long-term interests of the group(s)". 'Moving a group', 'some direction', 'produces movement', and 'long-term interests' are again all too vague to be of practical value for research or assessment and particularly unhelpful for team leaders seeking coaching. In addition, no reference is being made to what is going on in the minds of 'groups' that encourage them to 'move' in a particular direction. Again, this is too leader-centric. We agree, however, that team leadership is linked to 'non-coercive' means and this ties into our description of leadership as influence, both formal and informal.

Is Our Definition of Team Leadership the *Correct* Definition?

In any subject area, there are often several different ways of looking at an issue depending on what you are trying to explain. The key point is that the definition used should help in the search for explanations, descriptions, and forecasts. Our approach is to understand how team leadership *emerges* in organisations. In effect, we want to understand what is going on in team members minds when they willingly and enthusiastically accept their team leader's influence.

It is also important to point out that definitions, even in the natural sciences, are seldom perfect or set in tablets of stone. Anil Seth (2021) looked at the concept of human 'consciousness'. He tried to define what it **is**, a much more complex problem than trying to find out what 'leadership' **is**. He commented on page 14

> The history of science has demonstrated many times over that useful definitions evolve in tandem with scientific understanding, serving as scaffolds for scientific progress, rather than as starting

points or ends in themselves. In genetics, for example, the
definition of a 'gene' has changed considerably as molecular
biology has advanced.

This highlights that our definition of team leadership may be just a
temporary scaffold and it may well be modified and further improved
through research. But for now, we would suggest (and our experience with
team leaders confirms this) that it is a 'meaningful and adequate' and very
useful definition.

Myths, Value Judgements, and Ideology

Mats Alvesson shows clearly that one of the major problems with leadership
studies is that it is full of assumptions and value judgements. Leadership
is only used to describe 'good' outcomes and 'good' business outcomes
and uses value-laden terms such as 'authentic leadership'. Even the term
'transformational leadership' assumes that the transformation is good.
Alvesson refers to upbeat leadership theory, upbeat in the sense of positive
(meaning good). "Upbeat leadership theory typically includes a very positive
message about charisma, authenticity, transformation, servant-ship, sharing,
or something else, making the reader optimistic and disinclined to consider
a more realistic picture of organisations, work, and management (and this
leadership) in general…" (Alvesson, 2020: p. 3)

Mats Alvesson also suggests that upbeat leadership theory has more to do
with ideology than objective science. Alvesson (2020: p. 2) comments:

> Most leadership researchers define leadership as broadly 'good'
> implicitly for 'all'. If it is not 'good' then it is not leadership,
> but something like supervision. Given the complicated and
> multidimensional nature of social life, this one-sided positive view
> of leadership seems over-simplified and ideological.

ETL is only concerned with team members willingly and enthusiastically
accepting their team leader's influence. We do not claim that the outcomes
are 'good' – indeed the outcomes could even be immoral or a disaster for
the team, the organisation, or wider society. The implication is that many
leadership studies are far from objective and are more to do with promoting
an ideology, more in keeping with theology than a social science.

Science Should Be Value-Free

ETL aims to be value-free. A good example where values creep into the discussion of team leadership can be seen in the term 'authentic' leadership – a term used in many books. This term suggests that the leader must be true to themselves. As Anthony Gell (2014: p. 149) comments authenticity is "...the fine art of just being themselves".

Additionally, Fredrik Arnander (2013: p. 41) suggests to his readers that "Ideally, you are one authentic person".

But using terms like *authentic leadership* can lead to value-laden and muddled thinking. For example, perhaps those organisational leaders identified by Board and Fritzon (2005) who had some psychopathic tendencies were being true to themselves and acting like psychopaths!

Forecasts

We cannot make predictions in the social sciences because there are too many variables, so we attempt to make forecasts. We cannot control all the variables associated with the weather, so we *forecast* weather events, but we do not make predictions. We can make the forecast that where team leadership is perceived to exist by team members, then team performance will be better than if there was no team leadership perception. Forecasts look for facts and evidence; our explanation of leadership is 'meaningfully adequate', but we also need to support this in our case studies and research.

In a situation of perceived team leadership, we forecast that the team leader will have less difficulty in introducing innovation, improvement, and change compared with those who lack a profile of perceived team leadership. There will be less resistance to change with a profile of perceived team leadership because, by definition, team members are more willing to accept their team leader's influence.

In a situation of perceived team leadership, we also forecast that the team leader will find it less stressful or difficult to lead their team. If there is no situation of perceived team leadership so that the team do **not** willingly and enthusiastically accept their team leader, then the team leader, and perhaps the team, may experience stress, anxiety, frustration, and even conflict.

These forecasted positive outcomes of our approach to team leadership are *probabilities* based on what is going on in team members' minds, and as such, they are supported by meaningfully adequate explanations. As we have said before, just think about our definition of team leadership; would team members willingly and enthusiastically accept their team leader, if he or she was an incompetent manager who lacked knowledge and skill (expertise)? Would team members enthusiastically accept the informal influence of their team leader if team members gained no motivation or did not share values in their interaction with the team leader and did not see them as a coach or mentor, and did not experience socio-emotional rewards? Our explanation is thus 'meaningfully adequate' we understand and can relate to it.

Leadership and Business Success

In many books and articles, leadership is assumed to be linked to business success. Haslam et al. (2011: p. 124) highlight Meindl et al.'s research as far back as 1985 "…through an extensive archival study of over 30,000 press articles relating to 34 different companies…. revealed a significant and strong correlation between improvement in an organisation's performance and reference to leadership in the articles title". The implicit assumption being that leadership is directly related to or relies upon business success **to** be seen as leadership. Our definition of leadership is **not dependent** on business success, but it is **more likely** to lead to business success.

Even if the operational definition of leadership is achieved and people willingly and enthusiastically accept the influence of their leader, it does not necessarily mean that the leader and their team have the correct strategy and are moving in the right direction for the business or organisation. Business or organisational success is more to do with things like having the right strategy at the right time and the right resources to carry it through. However, what we do claim is that our definition of team leadership is more likely to lead to improved business outcomes because the team and leader understand each other and are fully aligned. Additionally, if the team perceive competence and expertise in the leader, it is more probable than not that the leader is competent and thus more likely to do the things that will lead to success.

The two research studies, Goleman (1998) and Fuda (2013), described in the next chapter, showed that an improved relationship between the chief executive and their team is linked to business success. Both studies used surveys of stakeholder opinions, whereas ETL just focuses on the team's opinions – although very specific opinions based around our 12 forms of influence. As you will see, both cases can be explained more fully by ETL, even though that is not the framework used by the researchers.

Avoiding a Tautology

The other important thing is that to design surveys which include the term *leadership* leads to a tautology or circular argument. As such, the result is not an explanation because all that can be concluded is that *leadership* is *leadership*. In science, you cannot explain an event by using the event in the explanation. You must separate the *explanandum*, what needs to be explained, from the *explanans*, that which contains the explanation. This avoids the tautology and separates what we are trying to explain from the explanation itself.

Conclusion

Our aim was to arrive at an explanation for 'team leadership', i.e., **What are the necessary conditions which are jointly sufficient for leadership to emerge in teams?**

We have arrived at such an explanation, and we believe it will have a hugely positive impact on the leadership of teams, as well as on coaching, training, and performance reviews for team leaders. Both logically, and in practice, if team members willingly and enthusiastically accept their leader's influence then there should be a positive correlation with high performance within the team.

Chapter 6

How We Arrived at the 12 Key Forms of Influence Found in Emergent Team Leadership

Studies That Have Helped Us Structure Our Approach

There is nothing new behind the 12 key forms of influence, they are all based on areas such as job satisfaction and employee motivation found in all books covering organisational behaviour. Nearly all the 12 forms of influence we outlined have been well-established for many years. What is new is seeing how team members evaluate their team leader and how those evaluations play a part in the emergence or not of team leadership as we have defined it.

Study 1: Herzberg, Mausner, and Synderman: Team Member Motivation

Herzberg et al (1959) separated those factors that created job satisfaction which he called motivators from those factors that if absent would cause dissatisfaction, he called these hygiene factors. The motivators were a sense of achievement for employees, feeling their work is recognised, having responsibility (today we might link that with empowerment), growth within

  DOI: 10.4324/9781003475569-6

the job, and interesting work. We cover many of these motivators in our discussion of social and emotional rewards.

When it comes to hygiene factors these were issues to do with pay, working conditions, company policy and administration, how employees are managed/supervised, fringe benefits, working conditions, status, and job security. We cover these in terms of the team members' perception of their leader's transactional forms of influence. There is a clear link between Herzberg's fringe benefits and our extrinsic incentives and how team members are managed/supervised when it comes to position, fear/anxiety, and how team members feel they are controlled.

ETL just looks at well-established previous research with an emphasis on team members' perception of influence both formal and informal.

Study 2: Bass and Avolio: Transformational and Transactional Leadership

Bernard Bass and Bruce Avolio have researched and written extensively on the topic of leadership and are some of the most cited authors in this field. In common with many authors and researchers, they did not define 'leadership', but instead used it to encompass a multitude of outcomes, and indeed they tended to stress outcomes and included value judgements. Their work (Bass and Avolio, 1990) though has been very influential on our thinking around the topic of leadership. They proposed 'leadership' as existing in three main forms: laissez-faire, transactional, and transformational. The latter form has become associated with what many people will view as 'leadership' and Bass and Avolio themselves saw this as the 'ideal' form of leadership.

Employee Perceptions

However, from our point of view, a key strength of their work is that they based their research on the **perceptions of employees** and their evaluations of leaders they had worked with. In their original research, Bass and Avolio (1990) asked employees to describe their best leader and their worst leader based on their experience. They then asked: What were the specific behaviours that would characterise such leaders?

■ Worst leaders were often described as 'blaming others', 'criticising team members', 'not supporting the team', 'managing by fear', 'working only for their own success', 'micromanaging', 'not praising good performance', 'not sharing knowledge', and 'creating rumours'. These can be seen under our transformational forms of influence.

■ Best leaders were often described as 'sharing information with others', 'interested in other people's opinions', 'gave responsibility to people', 'challenged ideas', 'organising things', 'long-term vision', 'good communicator', 'shares experience', 'shows proactive behaviour', and 'informed and competent'. Again, such perceptions are covered in our expert and reward forms of influence.

These behaviours are clearly relevant to what the employees Bass and Avolio surveyed and saw as important for 'worst' and 'best' leaders. But they are still based as much on the perceptions, interpretations, and judgements of those employees as on the actual behaviours of the leaders themselves. We would also suggest that these perceptions can themselves be viewed as responses by the employees to different forms of perceived 'influence' – both formal and informal – seen as emerging from the leader.

For example, in describing what Bass and Avolio (1998) call 'transformational leadership', the authors refer to the leader's values and principles, mentoring, coaching, and the leader's motivation. These we would categorise as team member perceptions of social and emotional rewards.

Value Judgements in Leadership

In our own ETL model, we do not necessarily see leadership as 'transformational'. The term *transformational* is a value-laden term and is seen as inherently 'good'. However, it is just as *transformational* to close a business down; or to lose a battle. In our own model, we instead refer to team members accepting the leader's influence and explaining why they do this, whatever the outcome or wider context of this 'leadership'.

Bass and Avolio (1998) also referenced 'inspirational motivation'. In our definition of leadership, we do see team members 'enthusiastically' accepting the leader's influence. However, whilst Bass and Avolio saw such properties as belonging to the leader, our approach is to see enthusiasm and motivation as a team-based reaction, owned entirely by the team; it may be the leader's behaviour that creates those perceptions, but it is the team member's interpretation that creates the reaction.

As noted above, their work also refers to forms of *transactional* leadership. It is often associated with formal forms of authority such as rank or position or when team leaders use financial incentives as a form of team member incentive. Bass (1999b: p. 5) commented that "Transactional leadership behaviour (from the team leader) caters to the self-interest of followers". We would suggest that 'self-interest' is a rather value-laden term and try to avoid such value judgements in our model. For example, we might wonder whether team members who seek social and emotional rewards such as shared values, beneficial change, the desire to be motivated, and having a leader who is interested in their training and development are also not engaged in some form of self-interest! However, we do note the general value of the term *transactional* as a very common form of influence and so have adopted it in our model.

Our Conclusions From Their Work

Our ETL model aims to avoid value judgements and is instead much more focused on teams and team members' perceptions, as well as being less leader-centric. We are not rejecting Bass and Avolio's research into employee's perceptions of good and bad leaders, but we are redirecting those perceptions into team leader influences.

Bernard Bass (1999a) suggested that the 360-degree questionnaire he developed with Avolio, the Multifactor Leadership Questionnaire (MLQ), was focused on leader's behaviours based on employee perceptions. A problem with 360-degree surveys, however, is that they tend to include all stakeholders including customers, so whilst that makes them wide-ranging in themes covered, they tend to lack focus and depth in terms of leadership. As in Chapter 2, our diagnostic instrument called the LPA goes only to team members to provide this focus and depth.

Study 3: Meindl: Leadership as a Social Construction

The idea that leadership is a social construction is not new. Ralph Stogdill (1974), in his review of leadership literature, referred to the possibility that leadership was an external attribution, not a 'quality' of the leader. James Meindl (1995) also rejected the 'leader-centric perspective' of most writers on leadership and instead proposed that the concept needed to be viewed as socially constructed. In his article, he does not propose an operational definition of 'leadership', but he refers to the 'romance' of leadership. "The romance of leadership perspective moves a researcher away from the personality of the leader as a significant, substantive, and causal force on the thoughts and actions for followers" (p. 330). This is in total agreement with our own approach; except we have proposed an operational definition of leadership and we do not use the term 'follower' or indeed the term 'romance' for considerations of team leadership – we are much more specific.

Study 4: French and Raven: Sources of Power and Influence

In their seminal work on power and influence, French and Raven (1959) identified five different types of 'social power': reward, expert, coercive, legitimate, and referent. These have become well-established mainstream terms, and we have therefore adopted them into our model although we apply them to the different contexts of team leadership and refer them to as 'socially acceptable influence' rather than 'power'.

We have also built on and expanded their five terms:

■ **Reward**. We use the term 'social and emotional rewards' that team members experience when interacting with their leader.
■ **Expert**. We use this term to reflect the concern of team members that their team leader is perceived to have some degree of managerial expertise or credibility.
■ **Coercion.** Whilst coercion, implying force, is not a form of commonly acceptable influence, we recognise that team members may fear or be anxious about their interaction with their leader, and as such it does act as a form of influence in a transactional sense.
■ **Legitimate.** We recognise the influence of this through the 'position' or job title held by the team leader and track this also within the transactional forms of influence.
■ **Referent**. French and Raven associate this with 'charisma'. Charisma may well be another emergent social property, but the concept of charisma is too vague to be included in our 'scientific' approach to discover what team leadership is and how *leadership* emerges in teams, so we do not include it in our model.

Bertram Raven in 'Social Influence and Power' (1965) included a sixth form of social power which he called 'informational power' – that is influence over others by controlling the information flow. We included this as a form of influence under the 'controlling' heading, although we have added more types of controlling behaviour commonly perceived by team members.

Study 5: Guirdham: Seven Factors Followers Look for from Their Leaders

Maureen Guirdham (2002: p. 545) made a list of seven of the factors that 'followers' (which we would associate in our model with team members) would have in mind when accepting a leader. This approach of focusing on what team members expect is very closely aligned with the approach we employ with our ETL model as below.

1. **Knowledge**: We address this as a form of expert authority or influence.
2. **Competence**: We also address this as another form of expert authority or influence.
3. **Status**: We refer to the title or position in the organisation within their transactional influence.
4. **Action to promote group goals**: We address this as organising/ planning as part of their expert influence.
5. **Identification with the group**: We address this in our shared values, within socio-emotional rewards influence.
6. **Motivation**: We address this in socio-emotional rewards influence.
7. **Appropriate communication**: Whilst not directly included as a form of influence in our model, our whole premise is that team leadership depends on the leader communicating with team members in such a way that team members recognise/perceive the leader's expertise, their provision of socio-emotional rewards and in some cases the transactional elements of their relationship.

Conclusion

We can see from our discussion above how we arrived at the 12 forms of influence described in ETL and the basis for the LPA diagnostic assessment. We have used accepted terms such as expert, reward, and transactional but have placed them in a different setting, the setting of formal and informal influence (authority) as perceived by team members.

We have also located, mainly through Herzberg and Bass and Avolio, much of the detail behind each of the 12 forms of influence. We have also added other forms of influence such as confidence (expert) because if team members felt that their leader lacked confidence this would weaken the team leader's credibility. Bass and Avolio also mentioned team members learning from their team leader. In recent years, there have been courses managers can undertake that strengthen their role as a coach, coaching their team members. We include this under coaching and mentoring. We have also noted that teams made up of professional and technical experts do not have to turn to their team leader for coaching and mentoring.

Chapter 7

How Other Researchers Have Approached the Concept of Leadership: Their Strengths and Weaknesses in Comparison to Emergent Team Leadership

Introduction

Many of the studies below seem to be moving in the same direction as Emergent Team Leadership (ETL). They seem to show that leadership emerges in teams and that there are links between their 'undefined' concept of leadership and such things as business success. ETL defines team leadership and arrives at a meaningfully adequate explanation of such links. ETL completes the picture and provides a fuller explanation.

Houglum: Emergent Leadership

David Houglum (2012) compares, what he refers to as traditional leadership, with what he describes as 'emergent leadership'. He states "Throughout the modern era, the western notion of leadership has been described using

DOI: 10.4324/9781003475569-7

words like 'predict', 'Plan', 'analyse', 'organise', 'direct', 'manage change', 'influence', 'vision', 'harmony' and most of all 'control'" (p. 25).

As explained previously, we totally agree as we have pointed out that such ideas muddle up what leadership **is** with its **purpose** or outcomes. He suggests that such an approach is teleological as we mentioned in Chapter 1. He also points out that the view of the natural science model is inadequate when looking at complex social issues such as leadership. But he does not then approach leadership from a **social science** perspective. He seems to have overlooked other social scientists who point out that social science aims for 'meaningfully adequate explanations'; therefore, it is not an explanation merely to look for *correlations,* as natural scientists do.

He concluded that the relationship between the team leader and the team is a 'servant relationship', the team leader is there to serve the team, and the team is there to serve the team leader.

He states on page 33

> The basic premise of servant leadership is that the leaders do not exercise authoritarian power and control to further their own agenda, but instead lead by being a servant first (Greenleaf 1977: 16). Through care, concern, and attention to the growth and autonomy of the 'whole person', servant leaders enable their followers to become servants as well.

Our model of ETL is also concerned with the **relationship** between the team and the leader and vice versa. From our perspective, Houglum seems to be looking in the right direction but has come up with another value-laden assumption, and one that is also obscure. ETL stresses that team leadership exists in the minds of team members; it is an **emergent social property** based on team members' perceptions of their leader's influence. ETL makes no value judgement about whether that relationship is 'authentic', has 'prescribed' outcomes, is 'transformational', or in the above case, is a 'servant' relationship.

In alignment with our own approach to leadership, however, what we do view as insightful about Houglum's approach is that he sees leadership as *emerging* through the interaction of the leader with the team. However, he then tries to merge what the leader **ought** to be doing with what he thinks leadership **is**. He seems to be trying to justify the servant leadership approach.

ETL leaves it up to the team leader to decide what his or her purpose or goal is as a team leader. What is key for us with ETL is that the team leader is more able to achieve whatever they want once the team is on their side and willingly and enthusiastically accepting their influence. Nowhere in this book do we say what a team leader **ought** to do once they are perceived in terms of *leadership* by their team.

Goleman: Emotional Intelligence and Leadership

Daniel Goleman (1998), writing in the *Harvard Business Review*, found a correlation between the financial performance of senior management teams and the fact that their leader, in this case a business executive, having above-average emotional intelligence. Emotional intelligence is abbreviated to (EQ) by Goleman and others.

Goleman concluded that "…my research, along with recent studies, clearly shows that emotional intelligence is the sine qua non of leadership" (1998: p. 94). The implication from this is that a necessary condition for the emergence of 'successful' leadership is when the leader has an above-average EQ. However, although Goleman did not have an operational definition of leadership, he seems to imply that it was somehow linked to the department's financial success.

ETL can explain *why* those team leaders with above-average EQs **are more likely** to be successful. We would suggest that because those team leaders understand that their team members have a desire to know what is going on and why. Those leaders with a high EQ are aware of how team members are evaluating them in terms of expert and reward forms of influence, they have empathy.

The description of emotional intelligence outlined by Goleman (1998: p. 95) describes the link, i.e., EQ has five key elements.

1. Self-awareness (hallmarks: self-confidence, realistic self-assessment, and self-depreciating sense of humour).
2. Self-regulation (hallmarks: trustworthiness and integrity, comfort with ambiguity, and openness to change).
3. Motivation (hallmarks: strong drive to achieve, optimism, even in the face of failure, and organisational commitment).
4. Empathy (hallmarks: expertise in building and retaining talent, cross-cultural sensitivity, and service to clients and customers).

5. Social skill (hallmarks: effectiveness in leading change, persuasiveness, and expertise in building and leading teams).

All these five elements would be expected to be underpinning many of the perceptions under the expert and reward forms of influence that make up ETL.

Goleman's research also provides evidence that indirectly supports ETL in that it shows a link, or correlation, between a leader's EQ and his or her team's financial success. However, our ETL model would suggest that a higher-than-average EQ is not in itself a necessary condition for this outcome. The real explanation, we would suggest, is that those with higher-than-average EQs may well be those team leaders who are **more likely** to have 'teams that willingly and enthusiastically accept their leader'.

In such cases, team members would perceive their leader with a high EQ as providing important forms of expert influence as well as socio-emotional rewards. As in Goleman (1998: p. 5):

■ EQ covers empathy: "The ability to understand the emotional makeup of other people and the skill in treating people according to their emotional reactions".
■ EQ also covers social skill: "proficiency in managing relationships and building networks and an ability to find common ground and build rapport".

From the team members' point of view, both are linked to their desire for socio-emotional rewards.

Goleman's article is headed 'What Makes a Leader?' Our answer is 'team leadership' is an emergent social property created by the team! The successful leading of whole organisations or businesses may be linked to the leader, the managing director or CEO, having an **executive team** that willingly and enthusiastically accepts their influence/authority.

Peter Fuda: "How Ordinary Managers Become Extraordinary Leaders"

In his research, Peter Fuda showed a clear link between the relationship a business executive had with his or her stakeholders and business performance. In the research, he used a 360-degree questionnaire which included the CEO's executive team as well as other stakeholders. Through coaching/consultancy, he also explored how the leaders perceived themselves and how the executive team and other stakeholders perceived them. His aim was to "focus on helping leaders transform themselves, their leadership teams, and their organisation" (Fuda, 2013: p. X). Fuda used a 360-degree questionnaire that concentrated on 12 perceived styles of leading.

- Constructive styles included achievement, self-actualisation, and humanistic encouraging.
- Passive defensive styles included approval, conventional, dependent, and avoidance.
- Aggressive defensive styles included oppositional power, competitive, and perfectionistic.

The perceptions he used were rather general when compared to our emphasis on perceived formal and informal influence. However, Fuda found that once he had given feedback to the leader so that they understood how they were perceived by their team, business performance improved. This is a similar process to that we recommend with our own approach.

However, Fuda committed two of the common errors we outlined in Chapter 1: he had no definition of leadership which could be measured and he conflated 'leadership' with business success.

As we have shown, ETL defines and measures team 'leadership' and is also more focused, with reference only to the relationship between the team and the leader rather than to other stakeholders. No doubt, after Fuda's coaching and consultancy, it is highly likely that team members 'willingly and enthusiastically accepted their leader', which is our definition of team leadership. In Fuda's case, the leader had a greater understanding of how the team, as well as other stakeholders, perceived him or her.

What Fuda also showed was that business performance seemed to be linked to the executive team leader and the executive team, as well as other stakeholders, **understanding** each other. In other words, as with ETL, Fuda noted the quality of the perceived relationship between their leader and their stakeholders as a key source of their 'leadership'. ETL is more specific as it pins down that understanding, or relationship, under the three headings of Expert, Reward, and Transactional forms of influence.

Haslam, Reicher, and Platow: The 'Social Identify' Approach to Leadership

A Broader Concept of Leadership?

In 'The New Psychology of Leadership' (Haslam et al., 2011), S. Alexander Haslam and colleagues linked leadership to the existence of a shared 'social identity' in the minds of 'followers'; the perception that they are an 'in-group', with a specific social identity.

Although they refer to *followers* which is a term we have avoided as previously discussed, their approach, like ours, sees 'leadership' as influenced by society and not as a quality of the leader. The latter aligns well with our approach to ETL as we have shown. The authors then refer to leadership through reference to all types of social groups, teams, and even categories of people such as voters as potential followers. Our approach would suggest that such a broad view is unlikely to lead to **explanations** (see Chapter 5); so we have instead confined ourselves to 'teams in organisations' so that our ideas can be tested. This does not detract from the potential importance of social identity (as highlighted in their in-depth findings) as an important factor, amongst others, when it comes to the emergence of 'leadership' in both social groups and in politics.

Indeed, Haslam et al. make a good case for social identity being one of the necessary conditions for what they describe as 'influence and power'. In ETL, we have concentrated on teams within organisations where the organisation labels the team and gives it 'identity' such as the finance team, the production team, the HR team, or the team of directors. This formal identity may be also added to by an informal identity or characteristic. In our explanation of leadership, the leader should be seen by team members as supporting the team, especially in front of more senior leaders.

Leadership and Influence

In their preface to their book Haslam et al. also state:

> Leadership for us, is not simply about getting people to do things. It is about getting them to **want** to do things. Leadership, then is about shaping beliefs, desires, and priorities. It is about

achieving **influence**, not securing compliance. Leadership therefor needs to be distinguished from such things as management, decision making, and authority. These are all important and they are all implicated in the leadership process. But, from our definition, good leadership is not determined by competent management, skilled decision making, or accepted authority in and for themselves. The key reason for this is that these things do not necessarily involve **winning the hearts and minds** of others or harnessing their energies and passions. Leadership always does.

This penultimate sentence really supports ETL.

Like Haslam et al., ETL sees competent management and the acceptance of our identified forms of influence as necessary conditions for team leadership to emerge. We agree that it is about achieving influence, not securing compliance, but it involves much more than social identity when it comes to team leadership.

In the extract above, authority is seen as less important than influence; although as is often the case with authors, authority and influence are not defined. The implication is that their reference to authority only refers to the authority given to the leader by the organisation. As we mentioned in Chapter 1, this overlooks the authority/influence given to the team leader by team members themselves, which we have shown is a very powerful form of influence.

You will also note that the term 'good' leadership is used, although 'good' is undefined and appears to be a value judgement. However, 'Winning the hearts and minds of others or harnessing their energies and passions', they infer, is essential for 'leadership', and ETL also focuses on these very things. Yet ETL is much more specific as we have an **operational definition** (see Chapter 5) and use terms such as 'willingly and enthusiastically accepting' the team leader, and we give examples of how such perceptions come about.

The Social Context

What is supportive of ETL in their social identity approach is the importance of the social context. Pointing out that the social identity approach is not entirely a psychological phenomenon, Haslam et al. state in their preface (2011: p. XX), "On the contrary, our approach is situated within the tradition that argues that the operation of psychological processes always depends upon social context. This means, on the one hand, that psychologists must always pay attention to the nature of society". ETL certainly looks at team leadership in the social context, it is one of our key premises that leadership is socially constructed. In addition, the perceptions of team leadership are adjusted by both society and the culture of the organisation and by the team itself.

The Importance of Perception

Haslam et al.'s preface (2011: p. XXI) further states "As psychologists, our focus is precisely to understand the nature of the 'mental glue' that binds leaders and followers together…". ETL has identified a 'mental glue' about what is going in on the minds of team members so that they willingly and enthusiastically accept the formal and informal influence of their team leader. For example, why do team members want to agree with, support, feel motivated, and in some cases, obey their team leader? Haslam et al. then go on to say (2011: p. XXI)

> For us, effective leadership is always about how leaders and followers come to see each other as part of a common team or group – as members of the same in-group. It therefore has little to do with the individuality of the leader and everything to do with whether they are seen as part of the team, as a team player, as able and willing to advance team goals. Leadership, in short is very much a 'we thing'.

In the Leadership Pathway Audit™ (LPA), we specifically refer, under one of the 12 forms of influence, to team members perceiving their leader as supporting or representing the team, but it is only one of the *necessary conditions* for leadership.

Terms such as group identity, 'in-groups', 'them and us', and the 'we thing' are very apparent in the political sphere where seeing the leader as 'one of us', having a common enemy or outgroup and using a scapegoat, is very apparent. ETL covers this in the importance of shared values, which can provide a powerful socio-emotional reward, but shared values differ in different social contexts. The idea of the in-group and out-group may only be relevant in the political sphere, and it is not always apparent with teams in organisations, and they are our focus.

Haslam et al. (2011: pp. 1–2) note

> …effective leadership is grounded in leader's capacity to embody and promote a psychology that they share with others. Stated most baldly, we argue for a new psychology that sees leadership as a product of an individual 'we-ness' rather than his or her 'I-ness'.

In many ways, ETL pins down the social identity approach and especially 'we-ness' by looking at social and emotional rewards. Specifically, this is highlighted through such things as shared values, team members seeing their team leader as interested in their coaching and development, and through seeing change as beneficial for the team as well as the team leader.

Explanations

The New Psychology of Leadership provides insights and certainly benefits from moving away from leadership as a characteristic of the leader, but it does not arrive at an operational definition of leadership, and by stressing one specific shared value it does not arrive at the *necessary conditions* which are *jointly sufficient* for leadership to emerge. As such, it does not arrive at an explanation (see Chapter 5).

In Chapter 3, Haslam et al. (2011: p. 45) state:

1. Whether or not leadership is successful depends on context.
2. Leadership is not a quality of leaders alone but rather of the relationship between leaders and followers.
3. Leadership is not just about existing social realities but also about the transformation of social reality.

On Point 1, whilst we agree on the importance of context, ETL does not refer to leadership being successful, we just concentrate on what leadership **is** and how it emerges, so we do not use the terms 'successes' or 'failure'. On Point 2, we agree that leadership emerges from a relationship, but we do not refer to *followers* but more specifically to teams within organisations. On Point 3, we also do not say leadership is necessarily *transformative*. To explain what leadership is, and how it emerges, leads to an **explanation**; to then say that leadership is also transformative is a separate issue and requires another explanation about how the introduction of innovation, improvement, and change is achieved. All we claim is that once the team 'willingly and enthusiastically accept their team leader' then innovation, improvement, and change are easier to achieve.

The key difference is that Haslam et al. refer to 'social groups', whilst ETL refers to 'teams' in organisations, where a 'team' is a specific form of social group. Social groups can include football fans and voters where 'social identity' is important, as it is the only 'glue' that helps to influence their behaviour. Teams, by definition, already have a shared identity amongst team members. The real value of the social identity approach proposed by Haslam et al. is that social identity is a powerful force in influencing people's behaviour in all types of social groups and that any team leader must recognise this if they want their 'social group' to accept them.

The Three Rs

Near the end of their book (Haslam et al., 2011: p. 205), they suggest a leader should think of three Rs, reflecting, representing, and realising.

- Reflecting: Observe and listen to the group in order to understand its culture.
- Representing: Ensure that your actions reflect and advance the group's values.
- Realising: Deliver, and be seen to deliver, things that matter to the group.

We came across the three Rs after we had designed our LPA but then recognised that in ETL and the LPA we specify and measure all three areas above. We specify **perceived influence** as an important part of team culture, we specify **shared values**, and we specify the type of things that matter to team members.

Epitropaki and Martin: Implicit Leadership Theory

Implicit Leadership Theory (ILT) is another theory that has many connections with our own approach. It has been described by Olga Epitropaki and Robin Martin (2005) in the following way on page 660:

It has been specifically suggested that organisational members, through socialisation and experience with leaders, develop ILTs, that is cognitive structures or prototypes specifying the traits and abilities that characterise an ideal business leader. According to Lord's (1985) categorisation theory, ILT's represent a recognition-based approach to leadership.

These 'prototypes', both positive and negative, are such things as sensitivity, dedication, charisma, attractiveness, intelligence, strength, dynamism, honesty, tyranny, and masculinity (see p. 660). These prototypes are based on what people would **like** their leaders to be. Epitropaki and Martin found that when the leaders in their study lived up to this image then the 'leader-member exchange' was more likely to result in improved "employees' organisational commitment, job satisfaction and wellbeing" (p. 659). We would argue though, as we suggest with ETL, that it is not surprising that if a team leader lives up to an employee's image of what a leader should be like, this leads to positive outcomes of the sort described above.

The strength of the ILT approach though is that it is based on employee's perception and what employees are thinking. However, the weakness seems to be using *leader* and *leadership* as words that mean the same thing – yet neither is defined, especially the concept of leadership. Also, they use general terms like *employee* or *followers*. ETL on the other hand defines team leadership and confines the discussion to teams. A strength of ETL is that team members themselves are asked questions about how they see the basis of their team leader's influence both formal and informal.

In the LPA, the term 'leadership' is not used in any of the questions as it might prejudice their response. ETL is simply based on team members' perceptions of influence.

ILT also came out of asking people what they think leadership represents. However, this is unlikely to be fruitful, as management thinkers and academics themselves have yet to come up with a common definition. The LPA avoids asking team members what they think leadership is, we simply ask team members about their perception of their team leader's formal and informal forms of influence, and we would argue that this reduces bias and confusion.

Conclusion

We conclude this chapter by saying that from the point of view of social science, ETL has validity in its approach. We have shown that our model has similarities to other 'models' of leadership but have also highlighted the distinct differences and how our approach seeks to overcome the conceptual and practical limitations of these other models.

In addition, we have also shown that whilst other 'models' of leadership link their approach to improved team performance, we can explain how this link would arise through ETL.

Chapter 8

Political Leaders:
The Context of Discovery

Politics and Leadership?

Emergent Team Leadership (ETL) is a paradigm shift, a new way of thinking about team leadership. It is not just another theory but one based on basic social science. The book's concern can be referred to as the 'context of validity'. The discussions in the book have aimed to show how ETL is a valid and useful approach.

The discussion below concerning political leaders is more about the 'context of discovery'. We are not political experts; we have not carried out political opinion polls. The diagnostic tool, the Leadership Pathway Audit (LPA), we have produced for team leadership in organisations would need to be radically changed when it comes to measuring political leaders and we would be measuring a different concept.

One of the changes might be to move away from the concept of political 'leadership' and replace it with how voters or the population judge or evaluate their political leaders. You will note therefore that when we discuss political leaders below, we will not use the term *leadership* unless it applies to the immediate team behind the leader.

The theme of this book is to explain and describe team leadership so that it is measurable and meaningful. We are never going to stop politicians, journalists, and writers from using the term 'leadership' in the political context. However, what we can do is to say to readers that whenever they

DOI: 10.4324/9781003475569-8

see the term 'leadership' ask themselves, what does the writer, journalist, or politician mean by the term?

In a political context, in most cases people use the term, 'lack of leadership', to mean such things as 'X politician has not made a decision', 'X politician has not made a decision they agree with', or 'X politician has not stood up to their own principles or values'. As we have seen, the term 'leadership' covers up many hidden value judgements and assumptions. In addition, if you come across the term 'great leaders' or 'great leadership' be very cautious.

But how do voters, or the general population, decide to support or reject those who stand for political office? We offer some thoughts below, but please note that the discussion below is very tentative as we have not arrived at an operational definition of a population's 'support' for their political leaders.

All political leaders, such as prime ministers and presidents, have a team behind them – in the United Kingdom it is called the 'Cabinet'. Also, political leaders such as Prime Ministers or Presidents will have members of their political party as members of Parliament, or representatives in the Senate or Congress as in the United States. The numbers of these members of Parliament/Senate/Congress will be large, but they still might behave in a similar way as a 'team'. However, it is really stretching the concept of 'team' to call them 'a team'. ETL explains the emergence of *leadership* in a 'team' around the Prime Minister or President, but it does not apply to the political support from the wider public, whether the leader is democratic or authoritarian.

Tentative Suggestions About Political Leaders

Our tentative discussion below uses holistic terms such as 'authoritarian governments', 'dictatorships', 'hearts and minds', 'voters', 'populations', 'culture', 'power', etc. We suggest that *culture* determines the nature of the leaders' power over any population. As we have argued with ETL, political leaders' authority is also socially constructed so that democratic leaders are generally followed by other democratic leaders, and authoritarian leaders are followed by other authoritarian leaders in alignment with the expectations of their country, culture, and history.

In Chapter 1, we suggested that to use the term *leadership* to refer to CEOs or managing directors leading whole organisations or to political 'leaders' is like trying to understand the term 'wave' by looking at the wave on the sea, radio waves, and the goodbye gesture all at the same time. They have some common characteristics, but they are about very different events. However, as we shall see below, there might be common elements when it comes to how people evaluate politicians as in the way they do with their team leaders. Firstly, both are socially constructed, influenced by culture. Secondly, political leaders may also be evaluated or judged on their perceived expert, reward, and transactional characteristics by the population. They might have different characteristics than those identified for team leadership, but the general headings might be similar.

We tentatively suggest that the same three mechanisms might be at work:

1. Expert evaluation (perceived managerial/political competence).
2. Reward evaluation (offering the voters or supporters socio-emotional rewards such as shared values).
3. Transactional evaluation (various forms of fear, control, extrinsic incentives, and position power).

The primary difference will be that political opinion polls will be asking different questions based on the three main areas above. However, from a scientific point of view, we might also initially have to use holistic concepts and be prepared not to arrive at 'meaningfully adequate' explanations.

Leadership of Teams in Organisations Compared With Leaders in the Wider Political or Social Sphere

We make a distinction here between teams in organisations and social groups or social categories such as voters. The three key forms of influence that create leadership in teams, i.e., expert, reward, and transactional still apply to the team behind the political leader, but what about the 'population', 'social groups', or 'categories of people' who evaluate or judge that politician?

We are suggesting that *categories* of people, such as voters, might accept the socio-emotional rewards of the politician (shared values), see the leader as competent (i.e., has expertise), or see some value in supporting that politician for transactional reasons, for example, the politician might offer financial incentives to voters (reduced taxes, etc.). The three key ETL forms of influence expert, reward, and transactional might therefore still apply to the perception of voters but in a very different way. Although please note that this is very speculative.

Another important point is that we have yet to identify the factors behind what voters are looking for. From our perspective a politician being supported by voters and winning elections is not leadership, as we have defined it, because it stretches the concept of leadership, and indeed what makes a 'team', far too wide, which then makes both terms meaningless.

Political Power and Fear

In some national cultures, the population may fear their political leaders, and this is clearly a transactional perception. Also, political leaders can use fear in a different way. As we saw in Chapter 7, Haslam et al. (2011) stress the importance of social identity and the creation of an in-group. For them, the in-group becomes more strongly identified if there is an out-group, and it is the out-group that is feared. Nearly all political parties want voters to identify with them and to fear the other political party, if there is one, getting into power.

Another common use of fear in politics is to identify a scapegoat, e.g., a social minority, foreign people, or other nations, who might be seen as enemies. Haslam et al. (2011: p. 105) comment: "As an aside, these are disturbing findings, because they suggest that leaders whose in-group credentials are insecure may feel the need to display prejudice towards out-groups in order to shore up support from their followers".

Historically, and even recently, politicians have invented or exaggerated an enemy to gain support. In some cases, the enemy was a legitimate enemy. For example, one enemy that was effectively used by politicians in the year 2020–2022, in Europe, was the pandemic virus COVID-19. Those politicians who were perceived to successfully fight the virus, mainly through a successful vaccination programme, gained popular support. Clearly, the virus was not an invented enemy.

Culture and the Characteristics of Governments

If we look at different countries, we could make the forecast that a change of government will not in itself bring about a change in the 'characteristics' of that government. In other words, one authoritarian dictatorship will be followed by a very similar form of government.

Interestingly, in Western Europe and the United States, there is a tendency to use the term 'regime' to refer to forms of government that are disapproved of; so we will use the neutral term 'government' because in science we try not to approve or disapprove. Science is concerned with what **is** not what **ought** to be or 'what we want it to be'.

In Russia, the Czar was removed in 1917, but ever since, the country has had various very similar forms of government. The long history of Chinese governments is also very similar. In the so-called Arab Spring (c. 2011), when several authoritarian dictatorships were overthrown, they were also very soon replaced by similar forms of government. The governments of Egypt, Syria, Libya, Algeria, and Yemen all showed one authoritarian government being replaced by another similar style of government. This would be forecasted by seeing political leader support as being socially constructed.

The war in Iraq, because it was about 'regime change', failed to lead to a more democratic form because political 'leaders', in that culture, are expected to be authoritarian. If you want to change the nature of government then you must change the 'hearts and minds' of the population. After the Iraq war, there was some attempt to change the hearts and minds of the population, but it failed – admittedly a difficult thing to do anyway.

Look at National Culture Not Political Leaders

Just looking at political leaders is leader-centric so we suggest that it might be more fruitful to look at the social or cultural background of each nation. Why do people support or vote for them, why is their influence accepted? Some political journalists have looked to voters/supporters to arrive at tentative 'explanations', in the same way as we have looked at team members to explain team leadership. But because political leaders seem to exhibit a vast range of personality types, morals, qualities, etc., many journalists have long since given up the quest of seeking some common quality when it comes to defining political leaders. So, instead, they look at the motivation of the voters and supporters which we would suggest is potentially much more fruitful.

Joshua Yaffa (2020) in his book *Between Two Fires: Truth, Ambition, and Compromise in Putin's Russia* commented in the book's prologue.

> I became convinced that the most edifying, and important, character of journalistic study in Russia is not Putin, but those people whose habits, inclinations, and internal moral calculations elevated Putin to his Kremlin throne and now perform the small, daily work that, in aggregate, keeps him there.

This view clearly reinforces the social construction approach; Putin's acceptability exists in the minds of those around him.

With reference to authoritarian 'leaders' their influence in the minds of the population may well be largely transactional, such as position authority and fear, but there also exist shared values. Those shared values may well be a willingness to compromise Oliver Bullough, reviewing Yaffa's book *Between Two Fires: Truth, Ambition, and Compromise in Putin's Russia* (2020), comments: "Yaffa's most striking achievement is to show that every compromise he describes is completely understandable, yet cumulatively their effect is disastrous. The plural of compromise turns out to be corruption". Compromise and corruption may well be the shared values – as social scientists we do not approve or disapprove we just point out what is!

Looking at political power, we see clear examples of how supporters might view the politician in terms of expertise (competence), rewards (socio-emotional), and transactional dimensions. When it comes to expertise, voters might support a politician who is seen as having the following: confidence, national and international understanding, organisational and administrative skills, and professional/political skills. When it comes to socio-emotional rewards, voters might be looking for shared values, beneficial change, as well as a feeling that they can learn from the politician, will feel empowered, and can celebrate success. When it comes to transactional influence, the politician might be 'respected' because of their job title, but also because they have been given power to control. There may also of course be 'fear' of 'out-groups' that they can leverage (see below).

When it comes to the team behind the politician, then ETL is clearly very relevant. Fear or anxiety can be seen in the following: 'If you do not support me, you will be demoted. If you do not support my ideas, you will be expelled from the political party. If you do not support me, you will not be part of my cabinet (i.e., my team)'. All of these were exhibited in 2019–2023 in the United Kingdom by both main political parties.

Propaganda Means Controlling Perception

With reference to the social category of voters, fear is used by labelling the opposition as the 'enemy', i.e., suggesting that voting for them will cause economic chaos, will mean giving support to some foreign power, will allow too many foreigners into the country, will mean you will be poorer or more likely to be unemployed, etc. All of this is designed to create the 'out-group' and strengthen the in-group as Haslam et al. (2011) proposed.

Politicians also use propaganda, image, and public relations to control the **perceptions** of the population. Politicians understand it is not their behaviour that is crucial, but how that behaviour is perceived and how their image looks. In the modern era of mass media, governments want to be in control. In 2022, President Putin invaded Ukraine, and he justified this to the Russian people by describing the government of Ukraine as a threat to Russia and that Ukraine was becoming too close to 'The West'. Inventing an enemy is always good for popular support. Putin needed to control the perception of the Russian people about his decision to invade Ukraine and in that goal, he was significantly aided by his unchallenged use and control of the mass media.

Our discussion of political 'leaders' therefore gives considerable support for the idea that what makes a political leader 'acceptable' in their country is socially constructed. Given this, what is an acceptable political 'leader' in one culture is likely to be unacceptable in another culture. But we are using holistic concepts here, not concepts that refer to what is going on in the minds of individual voters, so we have not arrived at an *explanation*. In addition, we have not arrived at an *operational definition* of political support/influence or power!

Conclusion

Whether authoritarian or democratic all governments reflect their culture. It may take several generations for the nature of governments to change. Removing a dictatorship or trying to create regime change ultimately means trying to change culture, changing the hearts and minds of a population.

Chapter 9

Testimonials and Final Thoughts

Support for Emergent Team Leadership

As we have seen, one of the errors in understanding leadership was to assume it was all about outputs and results. In our training and coaching experience, we have come across many team leaders, at various levels in organisations, who have been on 'leadership and development' courses and programmes. These were all about what the organisation expected the team leader to deliver. The programmes only touched on, or left out completely, how the team leader was to deliver these outputs **through his or her team**. At the back of the team leader's minds was the simple problem of how to get the team to support and work with them. Our definition of team leadership, where 'team members willingly and enthusiastically accept their leader' resonated with team leaders.

Our field research found an impressive positive support for Emergent Team Leadership (ETL), and the results generated by the Leadership Pathway Audit™ (LPA). The following testimonials were typical:

- "I found the feedback extremely useful."
- "Our leaders and managers really need this." Multiple sector quote.
- "More useful than other assessment tools."
- "I have adjusted some of my behaviour as a consequence."
- "I found it a particularly useful process which gave me insight into how and where I (and the team) can focus effort."

DOI: 10.4324/9781003475569-9

- "Much more sophisticated than I expected."
- "Very clear layout, really accessible and feedback was easy to get on with."
- "What was useful was it was objective and not just comments from the team."
- "Made me realise one size of leadership doesn't fit all."
- "Much more about the team and the leader's ability to adapt."
- "It would be good to do more of it regularly."

Or as one experienced team leader commented:

> I have been doing a lot of research into leadership and what makes me a leader and what makes me a better leader. A product I found called the LPA hit the nail on the head in just so many ways and it is actually quite exciting in how new and refreshing it is. The audit itself is much deeper and broader than the 360 audit and tells you in great depth just how your team that you lead sees you. In many more aspects than green, red, blue, and yellow personalities. This audit took me to a new level, and I can't recommend it enough. I now work with a team that 'willingly and enthusiastically accept me as the leader' not because of my position etc but because of how I now see the team and my role.

We have found that using ETL and the LPA on a general leadership training or coaching programme has a real impact on team leaders, it is part of the programme that is relevant to their needs.

ETL and the Sociology of Knowledge

ETL is a new way of looking at the concept of team leadership, it is composed of new ideas or new knowledge. But why are some forms of knowledge accepted by 'society' and others ignored or rejected? The sociology of knowledge is fully expanded in an early work by Berger and Luckmann (1991) in their book *The Social Construction of Reality*. As we have explained previously, an important part of ETL theory points out that leadership is a socially constructed concept and an emergent social property.

In the philosophy of science, there is a distinction between making statements about what 'ought' to be (a value judgement) and what 'is'.

We have not claimed that forms of influence 'ought' to exist we have merely claimed that such forms existed. For example, just look at all the job titles that exist in all types of organisations that refer to rank of position.

As Jeffrey Pfeffer, in his *McKinsey Quarterly* article (2016), commented: "Part of this discrepancy- between the prescriptions of the vast leadership industry and the data on what actually produces career success- stems from the oft-unacknowledged tendency to confuse what people believe ought to be true with what is".

As we have shown, the traditional approach to leadership looks at leadership in terms of some property of the leader (i.e., a skill, behaviour, personality, style, outcome, emotional intelligence, knowledge, strong interpersonal skills, integrity, trust, business success, mindset, etc.) and this approach then enables leaders to be trained in such 'leadership' skills.

Leadership 'development' is a huge and profitable business; Pfeffer (2016) put the figure in the United States as between $14 billion and $50 billion. Seeing leadership as socially constructed, at first glance, means leaders cannot be trained. The logical conclusion seems to be that we should train or coach team members, not the leader. Armies actually do both, so do bureaucracies, though less formally.

However, unlike other leadership books . . . .

■ We have arrived at an operational definition of team leadership.
■ With this, we can then measure team 'leadership'.
■ From this team leaders can then be trained or coached.
■ As a result of that, they are then more likely to be perceived in terms of displaying *leadership* by their team.

Interestingly, some of our colleagues thought our approach to team leadership would never get off the ground because there is a big business behind the traditional route of training leaders as if leadership were some 'properties' they 'ought to have'. We are reminded of Machiavelli, probably the first exponent of the sociology of knowledge, who commented on why new systems (such as our ETL model) will often struggle to be accepted.

Machiavelli ([1513] 1921) wrote:

It must be remembered that there is nothing more difficult to plan, more doubtful of success, nor more dangerous to manage than the creation of a new system. For the initiator has the enmity of all who should profit by the preservation of the old institution, and merely lukewarm defenders in those who would gain by the new one. (p. 22)

Some commentators find it difficult to break away from the traditional approach as seeing leadership as some 'property' of the leader. The experts in leadership are the military and in our field research with them they visualised leadership along the lines we have taken – they know that all types of officers and commanders exhibit 'leadership', so it does not depend on some 'property' of the leader.

Their model of leadership was developed by Sir John Adair (1973). His work suggested that leadership emerges when the needs of team members are met, the team is cohesive, and the organisational goals are achieved. ETL merely concentrates on team members' perceptions and narrows down Adair's broader approach. We piloted our questionnaire in 2020–2023 with the British Army and Civil Service. Such team leaders found it more relevant and useful than any other assessment system they had used. Results from the LPA were much more supportive of ETL than we had ever imagined.

Is ETL a Product of Its Time?

ETL is also a product of its time. In the sociology of knowledge, new ways of thinking and challenging old assumptions are themselves products of social change. Our model may well be the result of the development of self-managed teams and empowering team members. In many ways, we are empowering team members by looking at their perceptions. Team members are now important agents when it comes to understanding and explaining team 'leadership'. In organisational life, in the 21st century, 'society' is less elitist and more democratic. ETL is also socially constructed, but we can see that it also provides insight, understanding, and at the same time is potentially useful for all team leaders and those who support, coach, or train them.

Finally, we approached some publishing companies about publishing the book you are now reading, and a large minority seemed cautious because they had recently published books on leadership based on what that author feels leadership ought to be, e.g., honest, caring, insightful, socially skilled, etc. Our book, as you are aware, defines team leadership and shows how

it emerges in organisations and that team leadership can be attributed
to a team leader who may have none of the so-called qualities above. It
would be nice (a value judgement), if leadership were simply about such
'qualities', but objective science is about what **is**. Other publishers found
ETL 'too complicated', but new ideas often seem too complicated. When we
explained ETL to employees and leaders in organisations, their comment
was often "It all makes perfect sense".

Our approach is a 'paradigm shift', a new way of thinking, and an
example of disruptive innovation. We see ETL as compelling and ground-
breaking, but so far, our experience supports, what the economist John
Maynard Keynes (1936) said:

> The difficulty lies, not in the new ideas, but in escaping from the
> old ones, which ramify, for those brought up as most of us have
> been, into every corner of our minds. (p. viii)

Finally, we have adopted a scientific approach, and all scientific
explanations are tentative, so the term 'hypothesis' is used. There is no such
thing as 'truth' in science. As such, our definition and resulting explanation
of team leadership may well be improved, changed, or even shown to be
'less useful' sometime in the future, but we believe we are not following a
mirage, more a useful pathway. Even in the well-developed natural sciences
which use sophisticated technologies (as opposed to crude, but useful,
audits), explanations are still tentative.

We close with a letter from Ian Flintoff (Oxford) to the United Kingdom's
Guardian newspaper on 31 May 2021. His letter was a response to a
previous discussion that implied Einstein's theory of relativity could be
'wrong' as there were interesting developments in the discovery of 'dark
matter' in the universe.

Dr Flintoff states

> All such observations and conclusions are best qualified by the
> understanding that even our latest technologies (brilliant as they
> are), enhancing our five senses plus our intelligence and reasoning
> (evolved as the best we know on our planet), do not, in all
> likelihood, amount to a full or final perception of the phenomena
> in question. Human capacities -sensory and rational-with whatever
> ingenious technological enhancements, should not be assumed to

be even close to the truth of any phenomena. We are not, and will never be, omniscient.

He goes on to say that all new ideas are tentative findings. He closed the letter: "Perhaps Plato was right: we do not see things as they really are, but merely **as we see them**". So back to the importance of perception!

References

Adair J (1973) "Action Centred Leadership", Gower.

Alexander G (2010) "Behavioural coaching – The GROW model", in J Passmore, eds. 'Excellence in Coaching- The Industry Guide'. 2nd ed. pp. 61–72. Kogan Page.

Alvesson M (2020) "Upbeat Leadership: A Recipe for – or Against – "Successful" Leadership Studies". The Leadership Quarterly. https://doi.org/10.1016/j.leaqua.2020.101439

Arnander F (2013) "We Are All Leaders: Leadership Is Not a Position It's a Mindset", Capstone Publishing Ltd (a Wiley company).

Bass B (1999a) "Two Decades of Research and Development in Transformational Leadership". European Journal of Work and Organisational Psychology, Vol 1999, No 1, pp. 9–13.

Bass B (1999b) "Current Developments in Transformational Leadership: Research and Application". The Psychologist-Manager Journal, Vol 3, No 1, pp. 5–21.

Bass BM and Avolio BJ (1990) "The Full Range of Leadership Development: Basic and Advanced Manuals", Binghamton, NY, Avolio Associates.

Bass BM and Avolio BJ (1998) "You Can Drag a Horse to Water, but You Can't Make It Drink Unless Its Thirsty". The Journal of Leadership Studies, Vol 5, No 1, pp. 4–17.

Berger PL and Luckmann T (1991) "The Social Construction of Reality: A Treatise in the Sociology of Knowledge", Penguin Social Science.

Board BJ and Fritzon K (2005) "Disordered Personalities at Work". Psychology, Crime & Law, Vol 11, No 1, pp. 17–32.

Burns Robert (1785) "To a Louse, on Seeing One on a Lady's Bonnet at Church". https://www.scottishpoetrylibrary.org.uk/poem/louse-seeing-one-ladys-bonnet-church/ (accessed 26/08/24)

Chartered Management Institute research report (2023) "Taking Responsibility -Why UK PLC Needs Better Managers". REF Chartered Management Institute. https://www.managers.org.uk

Epitropaki O and Martin R (2005) "From Ideal to Real: A Longitudinal Study of the Role of Implicit Leadership Theories on Leader-Member Exchanges and Employee Outcomes". Journal of Applied Psychology, Vol 90, No 4, pp. 659–676.

Festinger L (1957) "A Theory of Cognitive Dissonance", Stanford University Press.

French JR and Raven B (1959) "The basis of social power", in D Cartwright and A Zander, eds. 'Group Dynamics'. pp. 150–167. New York, NY, Harper and Row.

Fuda P (2013) "Leadership Transformed: How Ordinary Managers Become Extraordinary Leaders", Profile Books.

Gell A (2014) "The Book of Leadership", Piatkus.

Gergen D (2000) "Eyewitness to Power: The Essence of Leadership-Nixon to Clinton", New York, NY, Simon & Schuster.

Goleman D (1998) "What Makes a Leader?", Harvard Business Review.

Guirdham M (2002) "Interactive Behaviour at Work". 3rd ed., Pearson Education Ltd.

Haslam SA, Reicher SD and Platow MJ (2011) "The New Psychology of Leadership", Hove (UK) and New York, NY, Psychology Press.

Heider F (1958) "The Psychology of Interpersonal Relations", New York, NY, John Wiley & Sons.

Herzberg F, Mausner B and Synderman B (1959) "The Motivation to Work", New York, NY, John Wiley & Sons.

Hollander EP (1995) "Organisational leadership and followership", in P Collett and A Furnham, eds. 'Social Psychology at Work'. pp. 69–87. London, Routledge.

Houglum DT (2012) "Myth-Busters: Traditional and Emergent Leadership". https:// Philpapers.org

Kelly S (2014) "Towards a Negative Ontology of Leadership". Human Relations, Vol 7, No 8, pp. 905–927.

Keynes JM (1936) "The General Theory of Employment, Interest and Money", Palgrave Macmillan 2007.

Kotter JP (1988) "The Leadership Factor", New York, NY, The Free Press.

Lord RG (1985) "An information processing approach to social perceptions, leadership perceptions and behavioural measurement in organisational settings", in BM Shaw and LL Cummings, eds. 'Research in Organisational Behaviour' (Vol 7). pp. 85–128. Greenwich, CT, JAI Press.

Meindl JR (1995) "Leadership Quarterly" (Vol 6, No 3). pp. 329–341. JAI Press Inc.

Meindl JR, Ehrlich SB and Dukerich JM (1985) "The Romance of Leadership" Administrative Science Quarterly, Vol 30, pp. 78–102.

Moldoveanu M and Narayandas D (2019) "Harvard Business Review March-April. Article Collection", Spotlight.

Machiavelli N (1513) "The Prince" Oxford University Press 1921 edition.

Pfeffer J (2016) "Getting Beyond the BS of Leadership Literature". McKinsey Quarterly, January.

Raven BH (1965) "Social influence and power", in ID Steiner and M Fishbein, eds. 'Current Studies in Social Psychology'. pp. 371–382. New York, Holt, Rinehart and Winston.

Reicher SD (2020) "Stephen Reicher is Professor of Psychology at St Andrews University Scotland and Co-Author of The New Psychology of Leadership with S Alexander Haslam and Michael Platow". Guardian, 6 July.

Ribbens G, Abraham M and Cumming A (2021) "Article in the Institute of Leadership". Edge, pp. 50–51.

Rosch E (1978) "Principles of categorization", in E Rosch and BB Lloyd, eds. 'Cognition and Categorization'. pp. 28–49. Hillsdale, NJ, Erlbaum.

Seth Anil (2021) "Being You: A New Science of Consciousness", Faber & Faber.

Stogdill RM (1974) "Handbook of Leadership: a Survey of the Literature", New York Press.

Whitmore J (1992) "Coaching for Performance: The Principles and Practice of Coaching and Leadership", Performance Consultants International.

Yaffa J (2020) "Between Two Fires: Truth, Ambition, and Compromise in Putin's Russia", Granta. Reviewed by Oliver Bullough 2020 1st Feb Saturday Guardian UK Newspaper Review.

Index

Printed in the United States
by Baker & Taylor Publisher Services